**Fearless Empathy Se**

# Achieve

# Balanced Personality

Unlock Your Unconscious Shadow, Confront Your Hidden and Rejected Self, Explore Your Integrated Growth Path, and Become a Complete Version of Yourself

**Devi Sunny**

## GRAB YOUR FREE GIFT BOOK

MBTI enumerates 16 types of people in the world. Each of us is endowed with different talents, which prove to be the innate strength of our personality. To understand the deeper psychology of your personality type, unique cognitive functions, and integrated personality growth path, you can scan the QR code below or visit www.clearcareer.in for a free download –

**"Your Personality Strength Report"**

# Successful Intelligence Series

1) Book 1 **Grow Practical Mindset**
2) Book 2 **Grow Analytical Mindset**
3) Book 3 **Grow Creative Mindset**

# Fearless Empathy Series

1) Book 1 **Set Smart Boundaries**
2) Book 2 **Master Mindful No**
3) Book 3 **Conquer Key Conflicts**
4) Book 4 **Build Emotional Resilience**
5) Book 5 **Develop Vital Connections**

# Clear Career Inclusive Series

1) Book 1 **Raising Your Rare Personality**
2) Book 2 **Upgrade as Futuristic Empaths**
3) Book 3 **Onboard as Inclusive Leaders**

# Contents

About the Book ................................................................. 5

Introduction ..................................................................... 7

1. Understanding Balance ............................................. 11

2. Hidden Side of Personality ....................................... 22

3. Personality One-sidedness ....................................... 33

4. Integrated Growth Path ............................................ 44

5. Shadow Work Techniques ........................................ 55

6. Balancing Self ............................................................ 66

Conclusion ...................................................................... 79

About the Author ........................................................... 81

May I Ask for a Review ................................................. 82

Preview of Previous Books .......................................... 83

Acknowledgement ...................................................... 105

References .................................................................... 106

# About the Book

Our Earth possesses enough resources to fulfill the world's needs, not the endless desires of individuals. Attaining a state of equilibrium in our systems could evoke a utopian vision. The rich have more than they need, while the poor lack essential resources. Striking a balance is an undeniable necessity. This can be achieved when creative minds devise innovative solutions to manage external resources efficiently.

However, it's crucial to recognize that humanity also possesses internal resources. These internal dynamics influence the equilibrium of external resources. Therefore, the question arises: Can achieving balance within ourselves extend to a balance in external resources?

Consider your own life. Do you consistently seek to strike a balance in various situations? Each person faces unique circumstances, leading to diverse natural preferences. According to MBTI, these preferences translate into personality types driven by specific cognitive functions, ranging from healers to inspectors, based on the intensity of love and power they exhibit.

In a world that rewards power, love often takes a backseat. Yet, those wielding power may experience constant tension.

On the same note, we all navigate through a spectrum of brandishing power and love, and an unbalanced life will be the consequence if we remain stuck using only one or the other throughout our journey.

To achieve balance, we must integrate the best aspects of all personality types within ourselves. How can we accomplish this? It is by understanding our shadow functions, ego, and the guiding functions of our unconscious and subconscious minds. Psychology provides solutions for a better life, and this book aims to explore the essence of some of these teachings and demonstrate their implementation in our lives.

Life is an ongoing journey, and though we encounter numerous experiences, specific meanings become apparent only at the right moments. Knowledge has the transformative power to alleviate our pain. Indeed, it may only sometimes be that we have the information we require at that moment. While no two lives are identical, all can universally apply principles, and theories can be shared for the benefit of all. The key lies in practical implementation, observing the outcomes in our unique lives.

# Introduction

**"We can be sure that the greatest hope for maintaining equilibrium in the face of any situation rests within ourselves."- Francis J. Braceland.**

Have you ever contemplated the intelligence inherent in nature, orchestrating the symphony of Day and Night with remarkable equilibrium? Could this cosmic balance be attributed to the precision of celestial entities in their designated orbits? Consider the Earth, steadfast in its orbit around the Sun— a feat dictated by its mass and intricately connected to what lies within.

The Earth's journey around the Sun holds profound significance, influencing climates that, in turn, shape our agricultural landscapes. Is our equilibrium not similarly influenced by this delicate interplay? Does balance not prove to be a crucial factor? And how can we ascertain our state of balance?

Balance is undeniably linked to a sense of peace and equilibrium. Imagine the tranquility that would accompany our lives if we adeptly mastered the art of balance. So, is balance not a fundamental necessity? The question remains: How do we recognize and achieve balance in our lives? What, indeed, is the essence of balance?

"The best and safest thing is to keep a balance in your life, acknowledge the great powers around us and in us. If you can do that, and live that way, you are really a wise man."
- **Euripides.**

Many of us are eager to seek solutions, yet the challenge lies in identifying where to find answers. A vast repository of solutions awaits us in books and web pages, ready to be explored and absorbed. In his profound insights on life, Carl Jung addresses a pivotal question—how to achieve balance—by emphasizing the integration of one-sided personality types through individuation.

Consider the notion of ego; it is not limited to the commonly perceived traits of arrogance, rudeness, or hostility. The ego is an integral part of our character, shaped over a lifetime as a survival strategy in response to our environments. When we elevate our values above all others, we risk becoming egoistic. This offense arises when our cherished values are challenged, leading to our criticism of people with different perspectives.

This defensive stance stems from our conscious allegiance to an idealized personality, rejecting alternative aspects or those associated with other personality types. Yet, these rejected elements persist within us subconsciously and unconsciously. Irritation surfaces when others fail to appreciate what we hold dear, and we unwittingly project onto them the aspects we have suppressed within ourselves. "There is no coming to consciousness without pain."

"The meeting of two personalities is like the contact of two chemical substances: if there is any reaction, both are transformed."- **Carl Jung.**

There are moments in our everyday lives when our values are called into question. This questioning arises from the ego we construct during our formative years, adapting our character to fit the demands of our early environment. We thrive in a friendly atmosphere that aligns with our personality type or ego. But when we encounter individuals vastly different from ourselves and choose not to retreat, true transformation occurs.

Throughout our journey, we cross paths with numerous individuals. Yet, some connections are memorable, marked by significant events—a major conflict, an intense romance, or a profound friendship. Each relationship is a teacher, imparting valuable lessons and contributing to our evolution.

"Whatever is rejected from the self, appears in the world as an event."- **Carl Gustav Jung.**

Indeed, we draw into our lives those individuals who play a pivotal role in our transformation. However, what do we become through this transformation? Deep within every individual lies a dual nature, a recognition of both favorable and unfavorable facets in our conscious and subconscious realms. Love (healing) and power (control) coexist within us. In navigating life's challenges, we often showcase our positive attributes to adapt and survive, not knowing that we must confront our darker facets when needed. Conflict emerges when we resist acknowledging and accepting our unconscious aspects.

"We choose not randomly each other. We meet only those who already exist in our subconscious."- **Sigmund Freud.** Nature strives to bring about our wholeness, akin to the constant transformations observed in the world. Life presents us with situations designed to foster learning and acceptance of our completeness. Now that we grasp the purpose of events as catalysts for transformation, why not cultivate a balanced personality with minimal resistance and pain? The concept of individuation offers a pathway to achieve this seamlessly.

"When there is clarity, there is no need for will." - **J. Krishnamurti.**

Those who tap into the power and love within can grasp this truth early in life. It's akin to harmonizing the Yin and Yang, the balance of Feminine and Masculine energies. This book explores achieving a balanced personality, preparing you to confront the challenges ahead. It equips you with the awareness to discern patterns and events in your life, facilitating transformation with minimal resistance and guiding you toward a harmonious and holistic existence.

# 1. Understanding Balance

**"Just as your car runs more smoothly and requires less energy to go faster and farther when the wheels are in perfect alignment, you perform better when your thoughts, feelings, emotions, goals, and values are in balance." - Brian Tracy.**

Israel, a small Middle Eastern country, shares a complex history shaped by religious and archaeological significance. With a population of over 9 million, primarily Jewish, the region holds sites sacred to Jews, Muslims, and Christians.

The nation's origins trace back to Abraham, acknowledged as the father of Judaism and Islam. King David and King Solomon, around 1000 B.C., played pivotal roles in ancient Jerusalem. Over the centuries, Israel saw diverse rulers, including Persians, Greeks, Romans, Arabs, and Crusaders. The Balfour Declaration in 1917 expressed British support for a Jewish homeland, leading to British control until post-World War II. The U.N. proposed a partition in 1947, creating Israel, but Arab rejection sparked the Arab-Israeli conflict.

The ongoing Israeli-Palestinian conflict has been significantly influenced by historical events such as the Six-Day War and the Yom Kippur War. Current tensions revolve around contested territories including the Gaza Strip, Golan Heights, and the West Bank.

The Zionist movement, advocating for a Jewish homeland, gained traction in the late 19th century. Israel declared independence in 1948, facing immediate challenges, including the 1948 Arab-Israeli War.

Clashes between Israelis and Palestinians endure, revolving around Jerusalem. Efforts for peace, like the two-state solution, face challenges. The U.S. supports Israel, notably relocating its embassy to Jerusalem in 2018. Ongoing conflicts, including clashes with Hamas, persist, with the latest war declared in October 2023.

The journey from a sacred origin revered by Jews, Muslims, and Christians alike to a battleground, what has changed? It's a clear shift from love to power over time. The place and the people are the same but with two contrasting potentials. "Where love rules, there is no will to power, and where power predominates, there love is lacking. The one is the shadow of the other." —**Carl Jung.**

Can balance be achieved in Israel from a scenario of no control to one of total control? It's uncertain, but balance begins with the people knowing the shadow within them. Where do we stand on the love-power scale? Is sustainability possible at both extremes? How do we reconcile our Yin and Yang? How do we balance our System 1 and System 2 thinking? Achieving equilibrium between creative and analytical intelligence - what does a practical solution look like?

**Evolution of Personality**

"The little world of childhood with its familiar surroundings is a model of the greater world. The more intensively the family has stamped its character upon the child, the more it will tend to feel and see its earlier miniature world again in the bigger world of adult life. Naturally this is not a conscious, intellectual process."- **Carl Jung, The Theory of Psychoanalysis (1913).**

We are shaped by our personalities from childhood, influenced by our environment and family. We often anticipate that a similar environment will align with our personality, but reality may expose us to different or opposing surroundings. Internal conflicts arise as we strive to navigate life with the personality we develop.

The ego formed to cope with a close-knit group now faces challenges when confronted with diverse environments. For example, balancing a predisposition for love in an environment dominated by power can lead to emotional imbalances. Individuals resistant to adjusting their personalities may experience considerable emotional strain, impacting their physical well-being.

It is crucial to recognize the need to adapt to various situations to avoid pain. Carl Jung wisely noted, "There is no coming to consciousness without pain." Imagine we consistently approach every situation solely from a stance of either love or power without adapting to evolving dynamics. In that case, our emotional well-being and relationships will be adversely affected when the dynamics shift. While acknowledging that power and love exist within us, the key is to be willing to navigate its spectrum.

Recognizing the shadow aspect of power when working from a foundation of love is essential. We can avoid becoming one-sided personalities by understanding and applying this awareness as needed. The ability to adapt according to situations becomes evident when we embrace the dynamic interplay between love and power in our lives.

**Balanced Personality**

A balanced personality acknowledges its conscious and unconscious elements, embracing strengths from various personality types without discriminating against values. Such individuals embody qualities ranging from empathy to effectiveness, giving to taking, sacrifice to seizing opportunities, love to power, letting go to holding on, humility to effectiveness, and non-influence to influence, recognizing the need for growth in opposing traits.

This balanced personality understands the importance of cultivating diverse intelligence, including creative, analytical, and practical abilities and developing these traits for success. For instance, empaths (N.F.s) can acquire the skill of influence to champion their values, while executives (STs) can utilize their influence to support empathic projects. It is essential for intuitive feelers to acknowledge that power is a tool that should be wielded when necessary, and utilizing influence is not a mistake but a strategic necessity. Power, in this context, refers to the ability to influence actions. From intent to implementation, it must be harnessed for effective action. If individuals perceive power negatively, they need to recognize its indispensable role in realizing the positive outcomes they intend. Power is not something to fear but a crucial means for enacting the goodness they strive for.

Dr. APJ Abdul Kalam's quote, "In this world, Fear has no place. Only strength respects strength," emphasizes the significance of strength rooted in respect.

"War is organized murder and torture against our brothers." "War is not the continuation of politics with different means; it is the greatest mass crime perpetrated on the community of man." "To all those who walk the path of human cooperation, war must appear loathsome and inhuman." -**Alfred Adler.**

Individuals naturally inclined toward influence and power, such as sensory thinkers, should comprehend that using their strength for the benefit of others leads to eventual success. They need to consider the broader impact of their power moves on others, as oppressing others for short-term gains may result in a detrimental powershift.

The wisdom in Takuan Soho's quote, "Preoccupied with a single leaf, you won't see the tree. Preoccupied with a single tree, you'll miss the entire forest," highlights the importance of maintaining a broader perspective and not getting caught up in singular aspects. It urges individuals to appreciate the interconnectedness of their actions in the larger context.

## Elements of Personality

Sigmund Freud's psychoanalytic theory proposes that human personality consists of three interconnected elements: the id, ego, and superego. The id, present from birth, is driven by the pleasure principle and seeks immediate gratification from basic urges. The ego, developing from the id, operates based on the reality principle and strives to satisfy impulses in socially acceptable ways. The superego, emerging around age five, encompasses internalized moral standards acquired from society and parents, guiding judgments and behavior. The interaction of these components is dynamic, with ego strength determining one's ability to manage conflicting forces. Freud emphasizes that a healthy personality results from a balanced interplay between the id, ego, and superego, while an imbalance can lead to maladaptive behavior.

"We are what we are because we have been what we have been, and what is needed for solving the problems of human life and motives is not moral estimates but more knowledge."- **Sigmund Frued.**

Carl Jung, a prominent figure in the history of psychology, contributed significantly to the field with his concept of Analytic Psychology. Initially associated with Freud, Jung developed his theories, incorporating ideas from natural laws and introducing personality types. His most distinctive contribution was the concept of the collective unconscious, suggesting shared structures in the unconscious mind across humanity, independent of individual experiences. He believed these archetypes were inherited and not learned, forming the basis of common reactions across cultures.

Jung's 'Theory of the Collective Unconscious' includes several common archetypes:

1. **Self:** The self represents integration and wholeness of the personality, serving as the center of the totality of the psyche.
2. **Shadow:** Signifies the dark, inferior, emotional, and immoral aspects of the psyche.
3. **Anima:** Portrays a strange, wraithlike image of an idealized woman, drawing the man into feminine behavior.
4. **Animus:** It serves as a source of meaning and power for women. It can be opinionated and divisive but fosters reflection, deliberation, and self-knowledge.
5. **Persona:** A protective cover or mask presented to the world to create a specific impression and conceal the inner self.

Jung's concept of dynamic psychic energy emphasized the balance of opposites in personality development, similar to the thermodynamic principle of entropy in physics.

**Personality Types**

Jung's influential work on personality types revolves around two primary constructs: attitude types and function types. Attitude types, introversion, and extraversion reflect one's orientation to external objects. Introverts withdraw energy from objects, seeking to avoid external influence, while extroverts extend energy towards objects, establishing active relationships. Jung suggests a genetic component to these temperaments.

The four function types describe ways individuals orient themselves to the external environment based on their introverted or extroverted tendencies. The first pair, thinking vs. feeling, involves intellectual vs. values-based decision-making. The second pair, sensing vs. intuition, relates to attention to external reality vs. incorporating a sense of time and hunches. Combining the two attitudes and four functions results in eight personality types, forming a cross of functions with the ego at the center. Jung's theory laid the foundation for personality assessments, leading to the development of the Myers-Briggs Type Indicator (MBTI). The MBTI, created by Katharine Briggs and Isabel Briggs Myers, incorporates additional factors related to lifestyle preferences, resulting in sixteen personality types.

The cognitive functions associated with each personality define their mental abilities, encompassing learning, thinking, reasoning, memory recall, problem-solving, decision-making, and attention. Primary functions, such as leading, assisting, supporting, relief, and ambition, influence our natural responses. Shadow functions come into play when dominant primary functions encounter challenges.

There exist eight cognitive functions:

Introverted Intuition (Ni), Extroverted Intuition (Ne), Introverted Sensing (Si), Extroverted Sensing (Se), Introverted Thinking (Ti), Extroverted Thinking (Te), Introverted Feeling (Fi), Extroverted Feeling (Fe)

Each of the 16 personality types uniquely combines these cognitive functions, profoundly shaping one's thoughts and actions. To grasp the psychology shaping your personality more profoundly, delve into the unique cognitive functions that further delineate it by downloading.

**"Your Personality Strength Report"**

https://clearcareerinclusive.ck.page/uniquegift

**Individuation**

By applying the concept of dynamic psychic energy to motivation, Jung posits that individuals are compelled to alleviate the disparity in psychic energy between conflicting emotions, like love and hate. Within this framework, personal growth towards completeness entails the comprehension and amalgamation of diverse or contradictory aspects within oneself and the broader world. Jung advocates for embracing diverse points of view internally and externally, as opposing views often contain elements of truth. He sees this as a path to forming a more comprehensive sense of self. A well-developed individual, according to Jung, is someone who can listen to and balance various points of view within themselves. At the same time, constant rejection of opposing perspectives may lead to imbalance and unhappiness.

"The conscious mind is on the top, the shadow underneath, and just as high always longs for low and hot for cold, so all consciousness, perhaps without being aware of it, seeks its unconscious opposite, lacking which it is doomed to stagnation, congestion, and ossification. Life is born only of the spark of opposites."- **Carl Jung.**

Individuation is the transformative process through which an individual becomes distinct from others, transcending the confines of the ego and the conscious psyche. This journey encompasses elements of the personal unconscious, influenced by the collective unconscious. Jung characterized individuation as the path to becoming a "whole" person, emphasizing that it involves a departure from societal norms, focusing on individuality. Despite this apparent separation, Jung highlighted that individuation fosters deeper and broader connections within the collective rather than leading to isolation.

According to Jung, the essence of achieving wholeness lies in successfully integrating the conscious psyche (ego) with the unconscious psyche. In contrast to some Eastern practices like meditation, which Jung perceived as misguided attempts to control the unconscious mind, individuation seeks a comprehensive unity—embracing ego, unconscious psyche, and community.

**Balancing Practice**

Identify your MBTI personality type, Natural Preferences, and Primary Cognitive Functions.

## 2. Hidden Side of Personality

**"I want freedom for the full expression of my personality." – Mahatma Gandhi.**

The movie "Joker" delves into the shattered psyche of Arthur Fleck, an unfortunate and confused man who grapples with a distorted reality shaped by a lifetime of physical and emotional abuse. His job as a party clown contradicts his inner turmoil, and he hides his emptiness behind makeup and fake smiles. Arthur's unpredictable laughter attacks, perceived as a disease or defense mechanism, stem from severe childhood abuse and neglect. The film masterfully portrays Joaquin Phoenix's depiction of Arthur's deep agony, making it a painful watch. Flashbacks reveal his delusional mother's ignorance of his suffering, contributing to a dualistic character torn between inner and outer worlds. Arthur's choice of a clown job, projecting happiness while suffering inside, serves as a coping mechanism.

The laughter, a reactive defense, shields him from the brutal outside world, simultaneously appeasing and repelling his delusional mother. Arthur's inability to distinguish reality from fantasy intensifies as he discovers his mother's psychosis and his adoption. This revelation marks his awakening and transformation into the violent, ruthless man he identified with during his abusive upbringing.

Killing becomes a means of becoming, shedding the illusions of a beautiful fantasy world. Arthur murders his mother, the anchor in his unreal existence, and eliminates anchors of hope in the real world. He kills those he cannot have or be, disconnecting from any semblance of societal norms.

In the end, Arthur becomes a product of his upbringing, a victim of parental wishes and actions, dead inside but wearing a big fake smile for the world. "Joker" is a haunting exploration of hidden personalities born from the scars of abuse and a distorted sense of reality, ultimately unraveling into a tormented and vengeful soul.

"The Psychiatrist knows that certain dangerous unconscious forces can be rendered harmless, or at least held in check, if they are made conscious, that is if the patient can assimilate them and integrate them with his personality."- **Carl Jung.** Confronting the shadow diminishes the potency of our flaws and weaknesses, preventing them from causing widespread havoc. Recognizing issues such as anger, selfishness, greed, aggression, obsession, or compulsion allows us to exert some control over these aspects. We can endeavor to overcome these flaws or mitigate their potential for harm.

**Hidden Personality**

Hidden personality is the mysterious part of ourselves that shapes our behaviors, often operating below our awareness. Sigmund Freud, a pioneer in psychology, believed powerful instincts and desires fuel our actions. According to Freud, we sometimes push these urges down, causing inner tensions and conflicts.

Conversely, Carl Rogers, a humanist psychologist, had a more optimistic view. He saw people as naturally positive, with an innate drive for self-improvement. Rogers believed that our true nature is positive, unlike Freud's emphasis on the instinct-driven, potentially aggressive side of human behavior.

Freud viewed humans as irrational beings driven by unconscious instincts, while Rogers saw rationality and a drive for fulfillment as inseparable. However, both agree on the existence of a hidden side to our personalities.

Carl Jung expanded the conversation by introducing the personal and collective unconscious. The personal unconscious contains forgotten or repressed elements from our unique experiences, while the collective unconscious holds shared elements from our evolutionary past. Jung brought forth the notion of archetypes, which are underlying patterns that shape and guide our thoughts and behaviors.

Stress is a revealing factor of our hidden personality, a phenomenon Jung termed being "in the grip." Stressful situations can bring out aspects of ourselves that we are unaware of, leading to actions that might seem out of character.

Jung's concept of individualization emphasizes an ongoing journey toward self-awareness throughout life. Instead of focusing on an unattainable endpoint, Jung saw personal growth and development as essential components of this lifelong quest. In essence, hidden personality is a complex interplay between instinct, consciousness, and self-discovery, influencing our actions in ways we may not always comprehend.

**Personal Unconscious**

In analytical psychology, the personal unconscious, coined by Carl Jung, contrasts the collective unconscious in Freudian theory. Often described by Jung as "No man's land," it occupies the border between the external spatial world and the internal psychic objective world. The personal unconscious encompasses elements not currently in conscious awareness but capable of resurfacing. It comprises contents that were once conscious but have faded from awareness through forgetting or repression. Similar to Freud's notion, Jung's personal unconscious involves memories that are readily accessible and those that are suppressed for various reasons. However, Jung views it as a "more or less superficial layer of the unconscious."

Within the personal unconscious, Jung identifies "feeling-toned complexes" as the constituents of psychic life's personal and private aspects. This conception aligns with Freud's idea of a realm containing an individual's repressed, forgotten, or ignored experiences. Overall, Jung's concept of the personal unconscious adds depth to understanding the unconscious mind by acknowledging its nuanced layers and the interplay between conscious and hidden elements.

One way the shadow becomes evident is through projection, where we attribute to others traits or qualities that we may unconsciously possess or deny within ourselves.

"Everything that works from the unconscious appears projected on others. Not that these others are wholly without blame, for even the worst projection is at least hung on a hook, perhaps a very small one, but still a hook offered by the other person."- **Carl Jung.**

**Cognitive Shadow Functions**

Myers-Briggs® personality typing explores the primary cognitive functions, the ego, and the shadow's role in personal development. Each personality type has a primary function stack consisting of four preferred functions in order of development and conscious power. They are Hero (dominant), Anima/Animus (inferior), Mother/Father (auxiliary), and Eternal Child (tertiary) functions. The ego is our conscious identity, often selective in showcasing positive qualities.

The shadow represents the dark and repressed aspects of the self, lying at the edge of the conscious and unconscious psyche. It contains primitive, negative, or socially depreciated emotions and impulses. Shadow functions can be both destructive and catalysts for growth. They become active during extreme stress when the usual coping mechanisms fall short. The shadow functions can be negative as individuals may lack conscious control over them, leading to irrational or morally ambiguous behavior. Recognizing and integrating shadow functions is crucial for personal development. Embracing and understanding these aspects can lead to growth, individuation, and a more balanced personality.

The shadow functions, also known as non-preferred functions, consist of four additional functions that are not part of the primary function stack. They balance and protect the ego. Inspired by Carl Jung's archetypes, the shadow functions are named Opposing Role, Critical Parent, Trickster, and Demon. These names reflect the roles these functions play in the psyche. Shadow functions, opposite to primary functions, emerge when one's ego is under threat. The primary Extraverted and Introverted functions are reversed to become shadow functions, influencing behavior in stressful situations.

1. **Introverted Intuition (Ni)**

Under stress, Ni grapples with confusion about perspectives, leading to a struggle to reach the correct conclusions. Fear of outcomes and self-doubt about noble decisions arise from overthinking numerous possibilities.

1. **Extroverted Intuition (Ne)**

Stressed Ne tends to misuse concepts without factual data, challenging decision-making. Driven by a desire to avoid conflicts, this function may lead individuals to act logically but insensitively toward others.

1. **Introverted Sensing (Si)**

Si keeps individuals in their comfort zones by relying heavily on past experiences, resulting in rigidity and resistance to new ideas during stressful situations.

1. **Extroverted Sensing (Se)**

In unhealthy scenarios, Se personalities may engage in excessive physical indulgences without considering long-term consequences for themselves or others.

1. **Introverted Thinking (Ti)**

Stressed Ti demands logical consistency and refuses to concede in arguments, fiercely holding onto and defending its position.

1. **Extroverted Thinking (Te)**

Te manifests as immediate, goal-focused behavior in a stressed environment, creating a pseudo sense of order. This function may lead to a lack of responsibility towards people, the environment, or resources.

1. **Introverted Feeling (Fi)**

Stressed Fi causes individuals to stand firm on what they perceive as correct, with little willingness to consider alternative views, making harmonious resolutions challenging.

1. **Extroverted Feeling (Fe)**

During conflicts, Fe may cause individuals to shut down to avoid further discussions, becoming cold and non-responsive. Focusing on self-protection during such situations can lead to neglect of others' feelings and expectations.

**Four Sides of the Mind**

CS Joseph discusses the concept of the four sides of the mind, delving into the intricacies of personality types beyond the typical four-letter MBTI results. He introduces the idea that each individual has four distinct sides of the mind—ego, subconscious, unconscious, and superego—each with its cognitive functions.

He breaks down the cognitive functions within each side of the mind, discussing the Hero, parent, child, inferior functions in the ego, and their counterparts in the subconscious, unconscious, and superego. The Hero, positioned at the apex of the conscious mind, represents the individual's primary and conscious personality. The parent, responsible and protective, guides the Hero by imparting responsibility and helping to avoid collateral damage. The inner child embodies innocence, and any attack on this function is likened to child abuse. It is essential to be cautious with the inferior function, where fear and insecurity reside. Interactions involving this function can lead to instant hatred as individuals strive to protect their security and sense of safety. Overcoming insecurity can lead to positive subconscious use, enabling individuals to channel their energy productively. He explores the significance of the inferior function as a gateway to the subconscious and how overcoming worry allows access to the unconscious.

Cognitive functions are manifested in the unconscious, subconscious, and superego, but with a notable distinction – they are inverted or flipped upside-down. Essentially, the four functions present in the ego have their mirror images on the opposite side of the mind. This duality results in 16 cognitive functions within the human mind. While there are eight distinct cognitive functions, each has its reverse mirror image on the other side of the mind.

For instance, consider the INFJ MBTI type, in which the primary cognitive functions include Ni, Fe, Ti, and Se. The shadow cognitive functions for INFJ encompass Ne, Fi, Te, and Si. They essentially adopt the cognitive functions of an ENFP as part of their unconscious realm. Moving to the subconscious or aspiring type, we find the opposite MBTI type, which, in this case, is ESTP with cognitive functions Se, Ti, Fe, and Ni. Furthermore, the MBTI type with the opposite functional pair transforms into the superego, and for INFJ, this would be ISTJ, characterized by Si, Te, Fi, and Ne cognitive functions.

In the case of an INFJ, Se functions as an inferior function, while Si takes on the role of the Demon function. Conversely, ESTP and ISTJ exhibit Se as the Hero function and Si as the Hero function, respectively. For INFJs, overcoming insecurities and fears associated with Se is crucial, as embracing Si into their consciousness allows them to navigate and understand the importance of identifying precedents. In this area, they may currently lack strategic approaches.

"If you hate a person, you hate something in him that is part of yourself. What isn't part of ourselves doesn't disturb us."- **Herman Hesse.**

### The Biological Blueprint of Personality

According to research highlighted by Christian Jarrett on BBC Future, personality traits like conscientiousness and neuroticism are strongly linked to our biology. Recent studies delve into the physiological aspects of personality, connecting it to hormones, immune systems, and even gut microbes. For instance, highly conscientious individuals exhibit lower stress levels, as measured by cortisol in hair samples, and maintain healthier lifestyles. Neuroticism, on the other hand, is associated with potentially harmful gut bacteria, shedding light on the connection between personality and vulnerability to illness. People who are high in conscientiousness tend to be **very responsible, goal-directed, organized, and responsible**. They make decisions carefully, are high-achieving, and stick to their commitments. People with high levels of neuroticism are **more likely to worry, exhibit emotional instability**, and perceive everyday situations as threatening or distressing and minor frustrations as hopelessly complex.

Additional research delves into connections between personality traits and indicators such as chronic inflammation, blood pressure, heart rate, and even psychopathy. As scientific investigations progress, the prospect of gauging personality through physiological measures like blood tests has the potential to transform our comprehension of the intricate interplay between psychology and biology.

**Balancing Practice**

Identify your Unconscious -Shadow Cognitive Functions, Subconscious and Super Ego Type, and Cognitive Functions.

# 3. Personality One-sidedness

**"The psychological rule says that when an inner situation is not made conscious, it happens outside, as fate. That is to say, when the individual remains undivided and does not become conscious of his inner contradictions, the world must perforce act out the conflict and be torn into opposite halves."- Carl Jung.**

Dr. Marty Nemko's article "The Psychology of Socialism and Capitalism: Toward Voting for the Best Candidates, not the Best Marketing Machines" in Psychology Today explores the psychological factors influencing political ideologies in the context of the 2020 election. The author delves into the contrasting perspectives of socialist-leaning and capitalist-leaning individuals, highlighting their emotional and values-driven inclinations.

Individuals with socialist leanings prioritize community, sharing, and collaboration, expressing a preference for redistributing wealth to promote greater societal equality. Their favorable attitudes towards government intervention and wealth redistribution manifest in supporting Democratic candidates who endorse free college, citizenship for immigrants, and equal access to healthcare.

In contrast, capitalist-leaning individuals prioritize rewarding success over wealth redistribution, emphasizing the core behaviorist principle that rewarding certain behaviors leads to more of them. They support free-market competition and merit-based approaches in various aspects of society, opposing higher taxes on the wealthy.

The author, positioning himself as a moderate, acknowledges the merits of socialism and capitalism. He expresses concern about the potential negative consequences of extreme redistribution and advocates for a balanced approach. The article encourages voters to be aware of the psychological underpinnings of their political beliefs, emphasizing the importance of aligning voting tendencies with personal values rather than succumbing to slick marketing campaigns.

"Achieve balance through the combined conscious states of the heart and mind." – **Steven Redhead.**

**Balancing Love and Power**

Scriptural teachings emphasize the importance of love and kindness in the context of our religious and cultural influences. However, the harsh reality of the world often reveals that dealings handled with love are frequently taken for granted, while human psychology usually places high value on exercising power. Those who cannot wield power are often perceived as having little value and are easily replaced by those who possess it. Empaths, Intuitive Feelers, and healers naturally use love in their interactions, often suppressing the power element within them due to upbringing or neuroscience.

Jesus, who never caused others any harm and instead based his actions on love throughout his life, presents an example of the consequences of choosing to serve with love alone. Jesus is revered as God due to his resurrection and victory over death. Jesus forgave the ignorance of his oppressors, yet he responded with a profound and impactful comeback. "If you want to see the brave, look at those who can forgive. If you want to see the heroic, look at those who can love in return for hatred."- **Bhagavad Gita.**

Empaths should learn to harness power not for harm but to cultivate self-respect and garner respect from others. It's crucial to discern whether one's love is rooted in fear, conflict avoidance, or consideration for the needs of others—a sentiment derived from empathy. However, it's equally essential not to fall into the empathy trap or become a doormat.

One must prioritize self-preservation before attempting to save others to determine if love is genuine and not driven by fear or an empathy trap. The ability to offer genuine assistance to others arises from becoming the best version of oneself, highlighting the importance of self-love. Without self-love, love for others may stem from dependency, insecurity, or internal lack.

Building influence is synonymous with acquiring power, defined as the ability to influence. For empaths, the objective should be to utilize this power for the benefit of others, aligning with the values they believe in. It becomes crucial for those who seek love to enhance their skills and competencies, extending their reach to build influence. Embracing traits essential for success, even if not naturally preferred, is critical to their effectiveness and competitiveness. Striking a balance between love and power becomes imperative for a holistic approach to navigating relationships and influencing positive change.

"Like the lotus flower that is born out of mud, we must honor the darkest parts of ourselves and the most painful of our life's experiences, because they are what allow us to birth our most beautiful self." - **Debbie Ford.**

**Power Or Ability to Influence?**

The terms "power" and "influence" often evoke visions of unscrupulous individuals employing Machiavellian tactics to manipulate people and events for their selfish gains, often to the detriment of others. Widely read books like Robert Greene's "The 48 Laws of Power," featuring chapters like "Get Others to Do the Work for You, but Always Take the Credit," further contribute to this prevailing perception.

Power represents the capacity of individuals to instigate change or exercise control over situations, events, and people. Frequently bestowed through official titles or positions, power is overt and conspicuous to others.

In contrast, influence operates in ways more nuanced and, at times, indistinguishable. It is the aptitude to guide others towards adopting your perspective, not through direct control as seen in power, but through persuasive efforts that shape their perception of a situation or concept.

The exercise of power often results in compliance, even if it is reluctant. Conversely, employing influence tends to garner consent, whether conscious or unconscious.

**Principles of Persuasion**

In his article in Psychology Today, "How to Use Power, Influence, and Persuasion for Good," Craig B. Barkacs MBA, JD, explores the concept of influence and delves into the Seven Principles of Persuasion, as articulated by Robert Cialdini, the esteemed author of "Influence: The Psychology of Persuasion." Cialdini's principles, outlined below, are widely regarded as foundational in understanding influence dynamics, though they should be seen as general guidelines rather than strict scientific laws.

**Consistency:** People generally strive to align their words and actions to avoid cognitive dissonance. For instance, individuals who express support for a cause in a small manner are more inclined to commit to more significant gestures. A classic experiment demonstrated that participants who had already committed to displaying small postcards in their windows were 400% more likely to agree to showcase unsightly Drive Safely campaign signs on their front lawns.

**Reciprocity:** A natural sense of indebtedness often arises when you give or offer something to others. A study showed that servers increased their tips by offering customers a small gift of mints along with their bills.

**Social Proof/Consensus:** Social beings follow the majority's actions in any given environment. In a well-known study, hotels increased towel reuse by 26% by informing guests that 75% of previous guests had reused towels during their stay.

**Authority:** Stanley Milgram's famous experiment showcased the powerful impact of authority figures when participants obeyed researchers' (played by actors) orders to administer potentially harmful levels of electric shock, underlining the influence of authority as a compelling force.

**Liking:** People are more likely to be persuaded by those they have a liking for. Various subfactors, including attractiveness, similarity, compliments, contact, and cooperation, as well as conditioning and association, contribute to an individual's likability.

**Scarcity:** The perception of scarcity drives people to desire what appears to be in short supply. This principle is evident in situations like pandemic-related hoarding, where the perceived scarcity of goods leads to increased demand.

**Unity:** Cialdini added this principle in his 2016 book Pre-Suasion. It emphasizes that individuals are more easily influenced by those they perceive as part of the same group or community. Marketing strategies, such as "Us vs. Them" and exclusivity marketing, leverage this principle effectively.

It is crucial to acknowledge that while these principles can be exploited for predatory and manipulative purposes, they can also be harnessed for positive ends. Understanding and applying these methods ethically can lead to constructive outcomes in various contexts.

"Look well within yourself; there is a source of strength which will always spring up if you are willing to look."- **Marcus Aurelius.**

**One-sidedness**

We are all works in progress with room for improvement. Much like trees shedding leaves to prepare for spring, there are always opportunities for renewal within us. Nature follows a pattern of growth and rejuvenation, and perhaps so should we. Consider the image of tame elephants; even as they grow into their strength, they remain bound by chains, often unaware of their true power. Similarly, we, too, may find ourselves constrained by the environments we inhabit, adhering to prescribed roles. To unlock our real strength, we must recognize the potential for growth in our personalities' hidden or rejected parts, providing an opportunity to reap the best benefits. With this realization, we can avoid being confined to our established personality types and natural preferences.

In the book "The Magic Diamond: Jung's 8 Paths for Self-Coaching," author Dr. Dario Nardi explains how all personality types can focus on integrated development by managing the challenges of the one-sidedness of belonging to a specific personality type and thus can develop themselves holistically over time. One can attain individuation by civilizing our unconscious cognitive functions (shadow functions). He writes, "According to Carl Jung, conscious and unconscious functions do not make a whole when one of them is suppressed." Individuation is a process or development course arising from the conflict between conscious and unconscious cognitive functions. He believes that as people mature, some obtain the privilege of the natural development of the opposite (shadow) function. For example, if a person favors the function' feeling,' they develop aspects of 'thinking' and vice versa as they progress in life and their respective type matures.

**Challenges of One-sidedness for Empaths**

Dario Nardi mentions how the 'Feeling' and 'Intuitive' cognitive functions of an empath face challenges brought on by one-sidedness.

**Feeling Cognitive Function:**

1. Empaths tend to make decisions based on their emotions. They are kind-hearted by nature and give less thought to facts and consequences.
2. They usually help others by considering the severity of their trouble and, as a result, not thinking about themselves to the extent that they unknowingly harm themselves.

3. Empaths value priceless values and are known to volunteer for compassionate causes, which makes them vulnerable to manipulation by evil people.

**Intuitive Cognitive Function:**
1. Empathic personality types play with concepts and possibilities in their minds. They are usually disconnected from their general surroundings and withdrawn from feedback received from their sensory environment.
2. They are usually known to be overly idealistic and optimistic and are not thought to consider practical difficulties.
3. These types are generally overconfident in their self-development and need help syncing with the actual state compared to their perceived state.

**How can we identify our areas for personal growth?**
Our personality type often reflects our ego—the values we vehemently defend when challenged, revealing its presence in our reactions. How do we foster growth once we recognize that an unchecked ego may hinder long-term progress? A key indicator is our emotional responses, particularly our appreciation or irritation towards certain situations. Upon closer inspection, we find ourselves entwined with our unconscious, subconscious, and super-ego tendencies, drawn to individuals embodying qualities we may lack or require for our development.

"There is a powerful force within us, an unilluminated part of our mind-separate from the conscious mind that is constantly at work, molding our thoughts, feelings, and action."- **Sigmund Freud.**

In the case of an INFJ, the need for Ne and Fi from an ENFP becomes apparent, as does an ISTJ's Si &Te and an ESTP's Se & Ti fulfill a similar role. These identified needs serve as growth functions for each personality type. Consequently, the cognitive functions requiring development in us establish an immediate connection with individuals strong in those functions.

Reflecting on our own experiences, individuals who have significantly bothered us may possess a cognitive function we lack or need to grow. Moreover, when we engage in criticism, projection, or judgment, it often stems from an irritation triggered by qualities in others that serve as reminders of aspects we have rejected within ourselves. This positive or negative dynamic aligns with the wisdom shared in the statement attributed to Jesus: "Do not judge, or you too will be judged. With the measure you use, it will be measured to you." It suggests that virtues and vices observed in others exist within us, and our environment influences our ability to conceal or reveal them skillfully.

"The shadow does not consist only of morally reprehensible tendencies but also displays a number of good qualities, such as normal instincts, appropriate reactions, realistic insights, creative impulses, etc.- **Carl Jung.**

**Balancing Practice**

Identify the one-sidedness of your type, the growth areas, and the corresponding cognitive functions.

# 4. Integrated Growth Path

**"Becoming integrated and whole is the spiritual path. The body is your vehicle. Your job is to learn about yourself from your experiences and change yourself. This is spiritual growth."- Gary Zukav.**

In the movie "Sense and Sensibility," the Dashwood sisters, Elinor and Marianne, embark on transformative journeys encapsulating the essence of integrated personality growth. Initially characterized by her composed rationality, Elinor undergoes emotional growth as she gracefully navigates unrequited love and disappointments. Her cognitive evolution is evident in her heightened perceptiveness of others' feelings and motivations, demonstrating a nuanced understanding of love and societal expectations. Elinor's unwavering commitment to moral principles and familial duty signifies her ethical development.

Conversely, Marianne, marked by her initial passion and romantic idealism, experiences emotional growth through intense love and heartbreak. Her cognitive maturation involves recalibrating her views on love and incorporating prudence and discernment. Marianne's moral and ethical development is characterized by a newfound empathy and a more considerate approach to relationships. The sisters' integrated growth is epitomized by their sisterly solid bond, supporting each other through challenges and learning from their strengths and weaknesses. As the narrative unfolds, the Dashwood sisters find a harmonious balance between sense and sensibility, recognizing the value of reason and emotion in their evolving perspectives. The romantic resolutions for Elinor and Marianne reflect their integrated growth, culminating in well-rounded individuals who have embraced the complexities of life and love.

The movie explores the conflict between emotions and common sense, showcasing the perils of letting romance and societal norms dictate choices. Elinor exemplifies common sense with self-control, while emotional Marianne faces deception and learns to balance her feelings with rationality. The narrative underscores the universal nature of love and the resilience required to navigate its challenges. Through Elinor and Marianne, the novel emphasizes the importance of balancing sensibility and common sense in relationships.

Pain catalyzes personal transformation and heightened consciousness. Experiencing heartbreaks prompts individuals to balance short-term decisions driven by the mind and long-term decisions guided by the heart. Achieving integration is a lifelong journey, and hastening the process may demand a higher price for consciousness. Despite an established growth trajectory, proper integration requires time and experience, often involving a spiritual process that dismantles the ego. Through this spiritual growth, one embarks on the journey to self-discovery.

## Wholeness or Integrated Self

Achieving wholeness is plausible in an ideal scenario where an individual possesses strength in all cognitive functions. However, acknowledging that everyone inherently has a dominant Hero and Parent function while the Child and Inferior functions may need further development is crucial. Growth in these areas requires time and appropriate experiences and can be challenging to achieve during the earlier stages of life.

Now, envision a situation where individuals team up with others who excel in their respective Child and Inferior functions. This collaboration embodies the essence of phrases like "unity is strength" or the concept of "united we stand, divided we fall." By leveraging each other's strengths, the collective becomes more robust and capable of addressing a more comprehensive range of challenges.

Considering that different personality types are associated with distinct intelligence, let's compare a family unit consisting of individuals with the same personality type versus one with mixed personality types. A family with the same personality type may have more cognitive functions and intelligence similarities. This homogeneity might lead to a more focused and specialized form of intelligence within the family.

On the other hand, a family with mixed personality types is likely to exhibit diverse intelligence. Each member contributes unique cognitive strengths and intelligence, fostering a broader spectrum of skills, perspectives, and problem-solving approaches. This diversity can enhance adaptability and resilience, as the family collectively possesses a more comprehensive range of capabilities.

"Unity, not uniformity, must be our aim. We attain unity only through variety. Differences must be integrated, not annihilated, not absorbed."-**Mary Parker Follett.**

Individually, we embark on a unique journey toward completeness, shaped by our distinct cognitive functions aligned with personality types. Our strengths and weaknesses differ, and with diverse intelligences, our experiences are equally varied. The unpredictability of interactions with different individuals adds complexity, eliminating the notion of a universal pathway.

Yet, the resistance to integrated growth, manifested by avoiding diverse circumstances and people, leads to stagnancy. The route to wholeness intertwines with the path to success. This journey involves the assimilation of intelligence derived from various cognitive functions. Renowned psychologist Robert J. Sternberg identifies Practical, Analytical, and Creative skills as the pillars of successful intelligence. Thus, the key to achieving completeness and success lies in embracing and integrating the spectrum of cognitive abilities.

"Integration is a basic law of life; when we resist it, disintegration is the natural result, both inside and outside of us. Thus, we come to the concept of harmony through integration."- **Norman Cousins.**

**Integrated Growth**

We all gravitate towards our comfort zones, seeking familiarity and easy connections with like-minded individuals. However, actual personal growth unfolds beyond these familiar boundaries. Embracing growth requires venturing outside our accustomed circles, where we encounter diverse perspectives and learn from experiences that challenge our preconceived notions.

In this journey, it becomes crucial to acknowledge and understand cognitive functions that may not come naturally to us. By incorporating these less familiar aspects into our cognitive repertoire, we open ourselves to a broader spectrum of knowledge and skills. Often, our early choices of primary cognitive functions stem from the convenience of staying within our comfort zones. However, as we confront the complexities of real-life situations, we realize that clinging to these preconceived notions can hinder personal development and fracture our egos.

For instance, recognizing the significance of sensory experiences becomes essential if you identify as intuitive. Similarly, if you tend to be a feeler, acknowledging the value of logical thinking is imperative. Rejecting one aspect in favor of another, such as favoring introversion over extroversion or vice versa, limits our understanding and growth. Embracing the diversity of cognitive functions enriches our perspectives, fostering a more comprehensive and adaptable approach to life's challenges.

"Wholeness is not achieved by cutting off a portion of one's being but by integration of the contraries."-**Carl Jung**.

## Integrated Growth Path

"The difference between the "natural" individuation process, which runs its course unconsciously, and the one that is consciously realized is tremendous. In the first case, consciousness no where intervenes; the end remains as dark as the beginning. In the second case, so much of the darkness is expelled that the personality is permeated with light, and consciousness necessarily gains in scope and insight. The encounter between conscious and unconscious has to ensure that the light that shines in the darkness is not only comprehended by the darkness but comprehends it."- **Carl Jung.**

The opportunity for growth of any personality type is dependent on the auxiliary function (Assistant/ Parent Cognitive Function) of that personality type. The Dominant (Leading/Hero) & Auxiliary (Assistant/Parent) Cognitive Functions make up the middle two alphabets of the 4-letter personality type.

Extraverts employ their primary function in external interactions, while utilizing their auxiliary function in their internal experiences. Since the outer world is of more importance to an extrovert, developing auxiliary functions helps them contemplate. While for introverts, the dominant function is used for their inner world, the auxiliary function should be developed to balance actions in their outer world. Personality Development is fulfilled if the auxiliary function is developed well to support the dominant function.

**The Car Model**

The Car Model, described best by *The Personality Hacker*, is a symbolic framework representing different aspects of one's personality based on the Myers-Briggs system. It conceptualizes the mind as a four-passenger vehicle, with each passenger symbolizing a distinct mental process. In the front seat, the Driver represents the dominant aspect of one's personality, the Flow State. The Co-Pilot, next to the Driver, embodies a less emphasized but crucial aspect known as the Growth Position.

The 10-year-old, situated behind the Co-Pilot, signifies a part of the personality with a push/pull dynamic named the Defensive Position. Lastly, the 3-year-old behind the Driver represents an unsophisticated aspect often overlooked until it causes inner turmoil, known as the Blind Spot.

The Myers-Briggs system introduces eight cognitive functions, categorized into learning and decision-making processes. Individuals have a favorite learning and decision-making process, creating a Driver and Co-Pilot. The choice between extraversion and introversion further refines this pairing.

For instance, an ENTP's Driver process is Extraverted Intuition (Exploration), and the Co-Pilot is Introverted

Thinking (Accuracy). The 10-year-old process is Extraverted Feeling (Harmony), and the 3-year-old process is Introverted Sensing (Memory).

Understanding these passengers in the Car Model aids personal development. The Defensive State arises when individuals resist acknowledging uncomfortable truths from the 10-year-old, either by shutting off external input (for introverts) or ignoring internal warnings (for extroverts). The 3-year-old, often neglected, can cause unexpected behavior during moments of stress.

This model encourages individuals to recognize, name, and integrate all aspects of their personality for a more comprehensive understanding and growth. The Car Model is a valuable tool for personality development, emphasizing the importance of building intimacy with each passenger.

**The Spiral Development of Cognitive Functions**

In Dr. Dario Nardi's book, "The Magic Diamond," he explores the developmental stages of the eight cognitive functions within each MBTI personality type. The following outlines the cognitive functions of MBTI personality types based on their developmental order:

1. Introverted iNtuition (Ni) - "Perspectives"
2. Extraverted iNtuition (Ne) - "Exploration"
3. Introverted Sensing (Si) - "Memory"
4. Extraverted Sensing (Se) - "Sensation"
5. Introverted Thinking (Ti) - "Accuracy"
6. Extraverted Thinking (Te) - "Effectiveness"

7. Introverted Feeling (Fi) - "Authenticity"
8. Extraverted Feeling (Fe) - "Harmony"

These cognitive functions play a crucial role in shaping the cognitive preferences of individuals, influencing how they learn and make decisions. Dr. Nardi's exploration of the developmental stages provides insights into the dynamic nature of these functions within the context of personality development.

**INTP** - *Ti,Ne,Si,Ni,Fe,Te,Se,Fi*

**ENTP** - *Ne,Ti,Fe,Te,Si,Ni,Fi,Se*

**INTJ** - *Ni,Te,Fi,Ti,Se,Ne,Fe,Si*

**ENTJ** - *Te,Ni,Se,Ne,Fi,Ti,Si,Fe*

**ISTP** - *Ti,Se,Ni,Si,Fe,Te,Ne,Fi*

**ESTP** - *Se,Ti,Fe,Te,Ni,Si,Fi,Ne*

**ISTJ** - *Si,Te,Fi,Ti,Ne,Se,Fe,Ni*

**ESTJ** - *Te,Si,Ne,Se,Fi,Ti,Ni,Fe*

**INFP** - *Fi,Ne,Si,Ni,Te,Fe,Se,Ti*

**ENFP** - *Ne,Fi,Te,Fe,Si,Ni,Ti,Se*

**INFJ** - *Ni,Fe,Ti,Fi,Se,Ne,Te,Si*

**ENFJ** - *Fe,Ni,Se,Ne,Ti,Fi,Si,Te*

**ISFP** - *Fi,Se,Ni,Si,Te,Fe,Ne,Ti*

**ESFP** - *Se,Fi,Te,Fe,Ni,Si,Ti,Ne*

**ISFJ** - *Si,Fe,Ti,Fi,Ne,Se,Te,Ni*

**ESFJ** - *Fe,Si,Ne,Se,Ti,Fi,Ni,Te*

According to Dr. Dario Nardi, the leading function (1st function) becomes the foundation of any personality type. As an individual matures, the focus should be on the development of its 2nd, 3rd, and 6th Functions for a rich and balanced personality. Further, the development of the 4th and 5th will manifest the greatness of the personality, while surrendering to the 7th and 8th functions will aid in graceful living.

For Example, an INFJ, in the process of learning, should use their assisting function as well as the growth function (Fe), which promotes harmony, the 3rd (Ti) function implying accuracy, and the 6th (Fi) function exemplifying authenticity in the above sequence.

Unawareness and unavailability of scientific information are major blocks to personal growth. This information, supported by Neuroscience, should help people choose the right approach for their personality types. Individuation, a crucial facet of human development according to Carl Jung, involves the journey of establishing a stable personality distinct from the influences of parents and society.

This journey towards self-realization is crucial during adolescence but continues throughout life. Jung proposed that individuation involves integrating various aspects of one's true self that may be lost or overlooked over time. It is an ongoing process that allows individuals to harmonize their evolving experiences and learning with their authentic selves.

**Balancing Practice**

Identify your integrated growth path and reflect on your current developmental stage.

# 5. Shadow Work Techniques

**"One does not become enlightened by imagining figures of light, but by making the darkness conscious. The latter procedure, however, is disagreeable and therefore not popular."- Carl Jung.**

Navaratri, an annual Hindu festival spanning nine nights, honors Durga, a manifestation of the supreme goddess Adi Parashakti. The festival is associated with diverse legends, one being the battle between Durga and the buffalo demon Mahishasura, symbolizing the triumph of good over evil. Celebrations encompass the worship of nine goddesses, recitals of legends, and chanting of Hindu scriptures. Ayudha Puja is an essential tradition during Navaratri, which involves worshiping tools and weapons. The festivities conclude on the day of Vijayadashami, marking the defeat of evil.

The spiritual significance deepens with the worship of Navadurga, the nine divine forms of Goddess Durga. Each day is dedicated to a specific incarnation, representing various energies. Commencing with Shailaputri, the embodiment of action and vigor, subsequent days introduce multiple manifestations of the goddess, namely Brahmacharini, symbolizing bliss, Chandraghanta signifying beauty, and Kushmanda, representing the creative power of the universe.

As the festival progresses, devotees encounter Skandamata, portraying the transforming strength of a mother, and Katyayani, the warrior goddess associated with a vibrant red, denotes conquering inner demons. Kaalaratri, a ferocious form with a dark complexion, points to acknowledging shadow aspects. Mahagauri indicates intelligence and peace, reflecting inner purification, while Siddhidatri, the giver of perfection, represents the integration of all elements in purple.

The progression through these goddess forms symbolizes a transformative journey and introspection. Navaratri intertwines cultural celebration with spiritual reflection and personal growth, offering a holistic experience. By celebrating these goddess forms, individuals engage in a symbolic exploration of their inner realms, undertaking a transformative journey and emerging with a better-integrated sense of self. The festival seamlessly weaves spiritual practice with psychological introspection, fostering personal growth and self-discovery through the symbolic journey into the various facets of the self.

**What is Shadow Work?**

Shadow work is a form of psychotherapy rooted in Jungian psychology that focuses on exploring and integrating hidden aspects of the psyche, often called the "shadow self." Carl Jung's concept involves acknowledging and assimilating positive with negative traits that individuals tend to suppress or ignore. The persona, representing the outward personality, contrasts with the shadow self, encompassing hidden, less desirable aspects. Jung proposed that the collective unconscious, encompassing societal memories and impulses, also contributes to the shadow, making systemic issues like racism part of this concept.

Engaging in shadow work entails the transformative process of acknowledging and assimilating the concealed facets of your psyche into your conscious personality. This profound process demands courage and a willingness to challenge the status quo, requiring you to step outside your comfort zone. Natural and organic, it unfolds when driven by a powerful objective to succeed or a genuine passion for the person you aspire to become. You are on a journey of evolving from your past self into a new and transformed version of yourself.

This evolution involves expanding beyond your current self to offer significant value to those you care about or to make a meaningful impact on the lives of others. Throughout the shadow work process, you may encounter challenges expressing yourself or periods of reflective silence, yet these moments are pivotal for personal growth. The choice between taking decisive action and engaging in introspection is influenced by your unique personality and the path of integrated growth you are forging. Embracing the shadows within leads to a profound transformation, enabling you to become a more authentic and empowered version of yourself.

"The greatest gift you can give somebody is your own personal development. I used to say, "If you will take care of me, I will take care of you. Now I say, I will take care of me for you, if you will take care of you for me. What if I become ten times wiser, ten times stronger, ten times better, ten times more unique? Think of what it would do for our friendship. The self-sacrifice usually earns contempt, self-development and self-investment earns respect."-**Jim Rohn.**

### Benefits of Shadow Work

As the concept of the shadow is inherently abstract and not easily quantifiable by scientific measures, its effects are subjective and context-dependent. What is deemed acceptable in one culture may be considered taboo in another, contributing to the fluidity of the shadow self.

Scientific research on the tangible effectiveness of shadow work remains limited. While empirical evidence is scarce, practitioners of shadow work report various anecdotal benefits. A report in *medicalnewstoday.com* lists the following benefits.

1. Identifying and mitigating negative personal traits, as well as those societal norms may have instilled.
2. Cultivating self-acceptance and fostering a deeper understanding of oneself.

3. Gaining insight into the challenges others face with their shadow selves.
4. Confronting and processing trauma, grief, and complex emotions.
5. Understanding the impact of societal influences, childhood experiences, and relationships on personal development.
6. Motivating positive actions, for instance, confronting implicit biases and channeling anger towards advocacy for causes.

While the scientific validation of shadow work remains a work in progress, many individuals attest to its transformative impact on their personal growth and overall well-being.

## Shadow Identification Steps

As suggested by Psychology Today, this simple exercise can be a starting point for recognizing and understanding your shadow self.

**Step 1:** Reflect on a person you strongly dislike or have negative feelings towards.

**Step 2:** List on paper all the traits, behaviors, or qualities about that person that trigger aversion or distrust.

**Step 3:** Take the same paper and write your name at the top.

**Step 4:** Acknowledge that the identified traits and qualities now represent aspects of your own shadow.

"Unless you learn to face your own shadows, you will continue to see them in others because the world outside you is only a reflection of the world inside us." -**Carl Jung.** We can also identify our unconscious shadow by noting what we are attracted to and appreciate in other people. You will have a connection to people having your unconscious ego and super-ego.

With people having your subconscious ego, you might dislike some of their traits because either you are not good at them or you see them as inferior.

For instance, INFJs may find themselves drawn to the shadow cognitive functions of ENFPs, as these functions become ingrained in their unconscious. INFJs may also admire and emulate ISTJs when their ego takes the lead. On the contrary, INFJs may be unsettled by the spontaneity, objectivity, and practicality of ESTPs. They may judge the ESTPs' ability to express themselves and their astute approach to navigating life and fulfilling their needs.

INFPs experience growth in ESTJ, developing an affinity towards the unconscious shadow cognitive functions of ENFJ. ISTP represents their super-ego. ENFPs, on the other hand, find growth in ISTJ, with ESTJ embodying their super-ego. Their unconscious shadow cognitive function is associated with INFJ. ENFJs grow in ISTP, ESTJs become their super-ego, and INFPs represent their unconscious shadow cognitive function.

It is crucial to discern the strengths and weaknesses inherent in each personality type and assign appropriate significance to their integration into our lives. Such awareness is vital for recognizing the qualities of each kind that are worth adopting. According to Carl Jung, individuals may benefit from the natural development of their opposite (shadow) function as they mature. For instance, if someone initially favored the 'feeling' function, they may cultivate aspects of 'thinking' and vice versa, evolving as they progress in life and their respective personality type matures.

"In the progress of personality, first comes a declaration of independence, then a recognition of interdependence."
– **Henry Van Dyke.**

**Shadow Work Methods**

Before delving into the techniques, it's crucial to understand why engaging in shadow work is indispensable. The negative traits and behavioral patterns residing in our shadow selves can sabotage various aspects of our lives – relationships, decision-making, and self-esteem. These patterns often stem from past traumas and experiences, shaping our responses and influencing our actions. By acknowledging, accepting, and integrating these suppressed aspects of ourselves, we can break free from their negative impact and attain a more authentic and fulfilling life.

Motivated by the insightful steps offered by Alexandra Tiodar, the principal author at Subconscious Servant, delving into shadow work becomes a profound and transformative expedition toward self-discovery, healing, and personal growth.

By implementing these seven shadow work techniques, individuals can unravel the layers of their subconscious, integrate suppressed aspects, and ultimately become the best versions of themselves. Embrace shadow work as a guiding light on your path to self-healing and self-acceptance.

1. Understanding and Knowing Your Shadow:

To effectively engage in shadow work, one must first comprehend the contents of their own shadow. Drawing from Jungian archetypes, individuals can identify their negative thoughts, emotions, and behaviors. By creating lists of recurring negative thoughts and behaviors and recognizing their triggers, one can gain insights into their dysfunctional patterns and wounded self. Understanding the shadow lays the groundwork for the subsequent steps in the shadow work process.

2. Reviewing Your Childhood:

A pivotal step in shadow work involves honestly examining one's childhood. By reflecting on the emotional and mental states at home, the relationships between parents, and the availability of resources, individuals can uncover the roots of their undesirable traits and behaviors. This self-inquiry allows a deeper understanding of how childhood experiences shape the shadow and influence present-day actions.

3. Noticing Your Shadow Operating in Your Everyday Life:

Once familiar with the shadow's negative traits, observing how it manifests in daily life becomes essential. Identifying triggers for adverse reactions and understanding the patterns that arise in various situations helps individuals gain awareness of their shadow's influence. This awareness is a crucial step towards replacing negative patterns with positive ones.

4. The "Projection Mirror" Exercise:

Carl Jung's concept of projecting disliked traits onto others forms the basis of this exercise. By examining difficult relationships and listing traits both despised and admired in others, individuals can uncover aspects of their own shadow. This exercise promotes self-awareness, revealing latent traits and fostering a deeper understanding of the self.

5. Shadow Work Prompts:

Utilizing prompts in journaling can be a powerful tool for shadow work. These prompts, designed to explore patterns, triggers, and trauma, guide individuals through self-discovery and healing. Clearing the mind through relaxation or meditation before journaling enhances the connection with the subconscious, where deep-seated patterns are often hidden. Explore over 100 profound shadow work prompts on *ScienceofPeople.com* to help you accept yourself and progress.

6. Healing Your Inner Child:

Acknowledging the impact of childhood traumas, inner child work becomes a valuable aspect of shadow work. Individuals can release negative emotions and patterns acquired during childhood by connecting with their past version. This process, often facilitated by therapists, aims to provide the love, acceptance, and support the inner child may have lacked, thereby breaking and replacing dysfunctional patterns.

7. Humbling Yourself:

The final technique involves humbling oneself to address the presence of a strong ego within the shadow. By examining judgments and biases towards others, individuals can gain a more compassionate understanding of diverse behaviors. This journey reduces ego-driven arrogance, nurturing humility and cultivating a deeper appreciation for the intricacies of human behavior.

Shadow work, while transformative, has cons, such as emotional overwhelm, misinterpretation, spiritual bypassing, and re-traumatization. To navigate these challenges safely, seek support from trained professionals or support groups. Set boundaries, approach at a comfortable pace, and balance with self-care practices. Prioritizing mental well-being during the process ensures a transformative journey toward self-acceptance and personal growth.

"Our shadows hold the essence of who we are. They hold our most treasured gifts. By facing these aspects of ourselves, we become free to experience our glorious totality: the good and the bad, the dark and the light." "Your life will be transformed when you make peace with your shadow. The caterpillar will become a breathtakingly beautiful butterfly. You will no longer have to pretend to be someone you're not. You will no longer have to prove you're good enough." – **Debbie Ford.**

**Balancing Practice**

Apply shadow work methods to address heightened egoism linked to a dense shadow.

# 6. Balancing Self

**"One day, in retrospect, the years of struggle will strike you as the most beautiful."- Sigmund Freud.**

INFJs, considered the rarest Myers-Briggs personality type, are known for their deep thinking, creativity, and altruism. However, a perplexing phenomenon exists within this personality type known as the INFJ door slam – a sudden and seemingly uncharacteristic withdrawal from interpersonal connections. When an INFJ is deeply hurt, betrayed, or overwhelmed, the door slam is a self-protective mechanism, marking a significant departure from their typical kind and caring nature. This abrupt shift raises questions about its nature, motivations, and potential reversibility.

The INFJ door slam is not spontaneous but is often a culmination of unresolved issues and emotional burdens. It serves as a boundary-setting mechanism to preserve the INFJ's emotional well-being rather than a mere act of holding grudges. In situations where continued interaction is unavoidable, INFJs may resort to an "emotional door slam," remaining civil but limiting emotional engagement to shield themselves from further harm. Understanding the reasons behind the INFJ door slam is crucial. It typically arises when an INFJ feels incessantly criticized or undervalued in a relationship, pushing them to end it to escape toxicity and drama abruptly. Highly sensitive individuals, INFJs require harmony, emotional support, and balanced exchanges in relationships. Reopening the door after a slam is possible, but it hinges on the other person demonstrating genuine remorse, understanding the impact of their actions, and committing to change. However, in cases involving severe damage, such as emotional or physical abuse, lying, or exploitation, the door may remain permanently closed.

"Until your personality has exhausted its obsession with running the show, your soul isn't given the space to express itself. Your personality can be threatened by your soul because your personality has controlled your life for a long time, and doesn't want to give up control. Your personality is like a wild horse that tries to throw off the rider trying to tame it. The rider is your soul." – **Corinne McLaughlin.**

INFJs often lean towards people-pleasing and conflict avoidance, leading to the suppression of authentic emotions and, eventually, the INFJ door slam. However, assertive and integrated INFJs understand the importance of setting boundaries, saying "No," and effectively managing conflicts, transcending mere accommodation. This shift signifies a move towards prioritizing self-expression, acknowledging personal needs, and maintaining emotional well-being. As INFJs evolve into a more assertive state, they cultivate healthier interpersonal dynamics, emphasizing open communication and balanced emotional exchanges in their relationships.

"Sometimes you have to do something unforgivable just to be able to go on living." "Whenever we give up, leave behind, and forget too much, there is always the danger that the things we have neglected will return with added force." "Man's task is to become conscious of the contents that press upward from the unconscious." "That which we do not bring to consciousness appears in our lives as fate." "The meeting of two personalities is like the contact of two chemical substances: if there is any reaction, both are transformed."- **Carl Jung.**

## Balancing Masculine and Feminine Energies

We live in a world full of energy, and understanding the spiritual forces within us is crucial. Masculine and feminine energies, often represented as Yang and Yin, play significant roles in our daily lives, affecting our mood, relationships, and overall well-being.

- **Feminine Energy:** This is fluid and associated with creativity, intuition, and empathy. It's about being. Activities like meditating, dancing, and spending time in nature can help cultivate feminine energy. Feminine energy is dynamic and passive, representing the unknown and internal emotions.
- **Masculine Energy:** This is logical and linked to rational, focused, and analytical thoughts. It's about doing. Taking risks, setting goals, and asserting

oneself are ways to tap into masculine energy. Masculine energy is action-oriented, external, stable, and logical.

Gaining insight into and finding equilibrium between these forces can pave the way for a life that is both harmonious and satisfying.

**Balancing Yin and Yang**

In mental health, the ancient Chinese philosophy of yin and yang offers a profound perspective on achieving equilibrium. Kendra Cherry, a psychosocial rehabilitation specialist, delves into this concept, exploring its relevance to mental well-being and its potential to foster peace, connection, and balance in our lives.

Yin and yang, symbolized by a circular black-and-white emblem, represent opposing yet interconnected forces shaping individuals and societies. These forces, known for their presence in Chinese culture, science, medicine, and spirituality, serve as a valuable lens through which we can understand balance in mental health.

Cherry breaks down the essence of yin and yang: Yin embodies negativity, passivity, and femininity, representing the energy of the Earth and moon. Conversely, yang embodies positivity, activity, and masculinity, symbolizing the sun's energy. These forces, though opposite, coexist harmoniously, emphasizing their interdependence rather than conflict.

The philosophy of yin and yang aligns with dialecticism, a set of principles rooted in change, contradiction, and holism. Cherry explores how these principles contribute to the balance between opposing forces, fostering harmony and interconnectedness in mental health.

Contrary to Western psychology's historical focus on the absence of illness, Eastern perspectives, influenced by yin and yang, emphasize a holistic approach. This approach considers the interconnectedness of physical, emotional, mental, relational, and spiritual aspects in shaping well-being.

Drawing from Eastern practices like yoga, qigong, Zen, and mindfulness-based meditation, Cherry illustrates the growing influence of these traditions in Western culture. Daoism, Buddhism, and traditional Chinese medicine inform these practices, promoting restoring dynamic balance in body, mind, and spirit.

Cherry contrasts Eastern and Western definitions of mental health, highlighting how the former emphasizes selflessness and integration with society and nature. The article explores research findings suggesting that people with dialectical worldviews, influenced by yin and yang, exhibit greater coping flexibility and acceptance of positive and negative emotions.

To integrate the principles of yin and yang into everyday living, Cherry recommends harmonizing acceptance with action. Embracing acceptance, reminiscent of yin, involves acknowledging the unalterable aspects of life, while embracing action, akin to yang, entails taking proactive steps for enhancement. Striking this equilibrium not only reduces anxiety but also nurtures personal growth.

The article also discusses balancing conflict with harmony, wants with needs, and autonomy with connection. By embracing forgiveness, empathy, compromise, and gratitude, individuals can navigate conflicts, manage desires, and maintain connections without sacrificing autonomy.

Cherry concludes by emphasizing that the goal of balancing yin and yang is not about pursuing constant positivity. Instead, it's about achieving contentment by seeking equilibrium in different aspects of life. In a world where balance is vital to well-being, the ancient concepts of yin and yang offer valuable insights for thriving and growing sustainably in our mental health journey.

**Balancing Personality Traits**

Our personality is a complex blend of stable behaviors, including thoughts, will, emotions, and inclinations. Personality is akin to a "molecule" composed of two key dimensions: temperament and character.

- **Temperament:** Innate and influenced by genetics, it's challenging to change. It involves physiological traits and emotional patterns. It shapes our inherited tendencies in behavior, thinking, and feeling.

- **Character:** Acquired through experiences, education, and culture. Changeable, influenced by actions and the environment. Subject to constant mental and environmental factors.

The interplay of temperament and character defines our personality traits, visible in our readiness to think or act in specific ways. Achieving a balanced personality requires ongoing effort, a lifelong process.

Personality traits significantly shape who we are and how we interact with the world around us. They often manifest in balanced and unbalanced ways, influencing our behaviors and relationships.

An article in FFI.org, catering to leaders of family-owned firms, lists the balanced and unbalanced traits along with vital steps towards a balanced personality. Here's a descriptive breakdown of some common personality traits:

**Antisocial:**

- **Balanced Trait:** Autonomous, courageous, self-sufficient. Individuals with a balanced antisocial trait can make independent decisions and confront challenges confidently.
- **Unbalanced Trait:** Aggressive, impulsive, disinterested in others. An absence of social balance may result in behaviors characterized by aggression, impulsive choices, and a disregard for the welfare of others.

**Narcissistic:**
- **Balanced Trait:** Ambitious, influential, confident. Those with balanced narcissistic traits possess healthy self-confidence and ambition, allowing them to inspire and lead others effectively.
- **Unbalanced Trait:** Arrogant, selfish, lacks empathy. An imbalance in narcissistic traits may manifest as arrogance, excessive self-focus, and a diminished capacity to understand the feelings and needs of others.

**Histrionic:**
- **Balanced Trait:** Empathetic, socially intelligent, friendly. Individuals with balanced histrionic traits exhibit empathy, social intelligence, and friendliness, fostering meaningful connections with others.
- **Unbalanced Trait:** Attention-seeking, manipulative, low emotional control. Unbalanced histrionic traits may lead to attention-seeking behavior, manipulative tendencies, and difficulty regulating emotions.

**Dependent:**
- **Balanced Trait:** Generous, reliable, affectionate. Balanced dependent traits include generosity, reliability, and affection, allowing individuals to form supportive relationships based on trust and loyalty.

- **Unbalanced Trait:** Excessive dependency, low self-esteem, indecisiveness. Unbalanced dependent traits may result in excessive reliance on others, low self-esteem, and difficulty making independent decisions.

**Obsessive-Compulsive:**
- **Balanced Trait:** Responsible, hardworking, methodical. Those with balanced obsessive-compulsive traits exhibit responsibility, diligence, and systematic approaches to tasks, contributing to their success in various endeavors.
- **Unbalanced Trait:** Perfectionist, inflexible, insecure, over-focused on work. Unbalanced obsessive-compulsive traits may lead to perfectionism, inflexibility, and excessive preoccupation with work at the expense of personal well-being.

**Schizoid:**
- **Balanced Trait:** Creative, self-confident, autonomous. Balanced schizoid traits include creativity, self-confidence, and autonomy, enabling individuals to express themselves authentically and pursue their interests independently.
- **Unbalanced Trait:** Emotionally cold, introverted, difficulty in relationships. Unbalanced schizoid traits may result in emotional detachment,

introversion, and challenges in forming and maintaining relationships with others.

Understanding the balance and imbalance of these traits can provide insight into our behaviors and help us navigate our relationships more effectively.

## Eight steps towards achieving a balanced personality

Achieving a balanced personality is an ongoing process that involves continuous self-reflection, openness to feedback, and a commitment to personal and interpersonal growth. The article in FFI.org also lists the following steps towards a balanced personality.

### Step 1: Self-Awareness and Growth Mindset

- **Recognize Personality Traits:** Acknowledge and understand your personality traits.
- **Take Personality Tests:** Utilize tools like MMPI-2 ( Minnesota Multiphasic Personality Inventory) or TCI-Report ( Temperament and Character Inventory) for insights into your characteristics.
- **Embrace Growth:** Develop a mindset focused on continuous personal growth and improvement.

### Step 2: 360 Feedback Process

- **Seek Input:** Engage in a 360 feedback process by asking colleagues, family, and friends for insights.
- **Use Reports:** Leverage reports from personality tests to guide and enrich the feedback process.

- **Professional Support:** Consider working with coaches or psychologists for external guidance.

### Step 3: Recognize Diversity in Personalities
- **Cultivate Attitudes:** Foster curiosity, humility, compassion, love, and perspective towards diverse personalities.
- **Personality Traits Spotting:** Actively recognize and acknowledge the unique traits of others.

### Step 4: Introspection and Courage
- **Face the Mirror:** Reflect on traits in others that trigger discomfort, using them as a mirror for introspection.
- **Practice Humility:** Approach this exercise with humility and courage to address unbalanced traits.

### Step 5: Curiosity in Understanding Others
- **Be Curious:** Take an active interest in understanding the personality traits of others.
- **Explore Contexts:** Observe how traits manifest in different contexts and how they intersect with your own.

### Step 6: Develop Social Intelligence
- **Cultivate Mindfulness:** Practice mindfulness to enhance awareness of your thoughts and feelings.
- **Label and Express Traits:** Develop the ability to label and express your traits appropriately.

### Step 7: Adaptation and Relationship Building
- **Adapt to Changes:** Cultivate adaptability to navigate environmental changes.
- **Build Strong Relationships:** Foster strong and loving relationships with those around you.

### Step 8: Alignment with True Self
- **In Tune with True Self:** Strive to align with your true self by being creative and at peace.
- **Psychological Health:** Work towards psychological health to promote a positive family climate and business success.

### Balancing Duality

In a world as labeled as ours, we're often told who to be and what to do from the moment we're born. But as we grow up, those labels can feel too constricting. The idea of duality says you don't have to be just one thing—you can find balance in being different simultaneously. Duality is about breaking free from strict labels. It says you can be many things at once. Dr. Logan Jones, a therapist, encourages shedding labels that don't fit and discovering your true self. You have the power to choose who you become.

Duality means embracing two sides of yourself. Here are three examples:

1. **Soft and Strong:** You can be sensitive while being strong. Like water, which is smooth but can wear away rock, being in touch with your feelings shows maturity.

2. **Healing and Whole:** It doesn't make you broken if you've been through tough times. Healing is a journey to reveal the wonderful person you already are.
3. **Calm and Powerful:** You don't have to be loud to make a difference. Being relaxed and steady, like leaders such as Martin Luther King Jr. and Gandhi, can bring decisive change.

**Balancing Practice**

Identify your predisposition towards specific personality traits and energies to implement methods promoting balance.

# Conclusion

Life would be more straightforward if one had the luxury of a personal assistant to guide our reactions and suggest appropriate actions at every juncture. While the prospect of developments in AI potentially providing such assistance might loom shortly, we must cultivate a fundamental understanding of ourselves and human psychology. As this book emphasizes, our behaviors stem primarily from our personality inclinations, influenced by our upbringing and environment—a realm where our control is limited. However, it is indeed wise to navigate life adeptly, steering clear of potential pitfalls and channeling our energy towards growth.

This book endeavors to compile information that can catalyze your growth with optimal efficiency. Life is a delicate balance between serving oneself and others to the fullest. We can only affirm that we've given our best and be satisfied, as success is comprehended only over time by looking back. Yet, more often than not, the path remains unclear, and the necessary steps are elusive. As the journey unfolds, we can only gather information to piece together the puzzle and connect the dots. Relevant books can provide essential insights that will assist you on your journey of self-realization.

## GRAB YOUR FREE GIFT BOOK

MBTI enumerates 16 types of people in the world. Each of us is endowed with different talents, which prove to be the innate strength of our personality. To understand the deeper psychology of your personality type, unique cognitive functions, and integrated personality growth path, visit www.clearcareer.in for a free download –

**"Your Personality Strength Report"**

# About the Author

Devi Sunny, a passionate author and mentor, has been fortunate to create the series: 'Clear Career Inclusive,' 'Fearless Empathy,' and 'Successful Intelligence.' She nurtures inclusive spaces, fosters empathetic leadership, and encourages cognitive growth. At Clear Career, she strives to offer guidance based on her experiences. If seeking supportive career insights, please reach out at contact@clearcareer.in.

# May I Ask for a Review

Thank you for taking out time to read this book. Reviews are the essential for any author. I look forward to your feedback and reviews for this book. I welcome your inputs to incorporate in and deliver an even better book in my next attempt in the very near future. Please write to me at:

**contact@clearcareer.in**

Your support will help me to reach out to more people. Thanks for supporting my work. I'd love to see your review and feel free to contact me for any clarifications.

# Preview of Previous Books

**Successful Intelligence Series**

**Book 1: Grow Practical Mindset**

**Are you prepared to elevate your adaptability, enhance practical problem-solving skills, and refine your judgment with practical intelligence?**

Unlock the keys to practical intelligence with 'Grow Practical Mindset,' the inaugural book in the 'Successful Intelligence' series. <u>Delve into the foundational principles of Sternberg's Triarchic Theory</u>, focusing on adaptability and problem-solving skills crucial for success across diverse scenarios.
*From practical exercises to insightful strategies, this book equips you with actionable tools to enhance decision-making in your daily life, empowering you to thrive in various environments.* This book will take you on an exhilarating journey through the following key topics, unraveling intriguing insights-

1. Practical Mindset
2. Triarchic Theory of Intelligence
3. Practical Intelligence
4. Examples of Practical Intelligence
5. 12 Traits for a Practical Mindset
6. Personality Types Natural Preferences
7. Cognitive Functions
8. Personality Growth
9. Fixed Mindset
10. How to Overcome a Fixed Mindset
11. Balancing Fixed and Growth Mindset
12. Growth Mindset
13. Right Environment
14. Courage Building
15. Mindset Growth Through Personality Awareness

16. Components and Strategies for Growth Mindset
17. The Growth Mindset: Examples for Practical Mindset of Idealists
18. What is Intelligent Thinking?
19. Types of Thinking
20. Cognitive Thinking Pattern of Idealists
21. Integrative Thinking
22. Adaptive Intelligence Beyond Cognitive Agility
23. AI-Enabled Integrative Thinking
24. Why do some ideas fail?
25. Top Five Traits of Successful Startup Founders
26. Cognitive Functions Ti and Te
27. How to Develop Ti
28. How to Develop Te
29. Idealists in Business
30. Navigating Innovation Realities for Business Success
31. What is Excellence?
32. Personality Diversity for Team Success
33. How do you choose the right opportunity?
34. Cognitive Functions Se and Si
35. How to Develop Se
36. How to Develop Si

Elevate your adaptability and master the art of practical intelligence with this indispensable resource that offers tangible solutions and real-world applications.

**Book 2: Grow Analytical Mindset**

**Are you seeking to sharpen your cognitive prowess, refine critical thinking, and unravel complex problems effortlessly through analytical intelligence?**

Journey into the depths of cognition with 'Grow Analytical Mindset,' the second installment in the 'Successful Intelligence' series. Immerse yourself in Sternberg's Triarchic Theory, **exploring the nuances of analytical**

**intelligence—refining critical thinking, problem-solving, and logical reasoning.** *Unlock expert strategies and exercises designed to sharpen your cognitive abilities, enabling you to dissect complexities easily.* This book will take you on an exhilarating journey through the following key topics, unraveling intriguing insights-

1. Analytical Mindset
2. Triarchic Theory of Intelligence
3. Analytical Intelligence
4. Applying Analytical Intelligence
5. Analytical Intelligence for Business Success
6. Personality Types and Cognitive Functions
7. System 1 and System 2 Thinking
8. Primary Cognitive Thinking Pattern of Idealists
9. Integrated Personality Development for Idealists
10. Power of Fast and Slow Thinking in Decision-Making
11. Fast Thinking and Purchase Decisions
12. Leveraging Fast Thinking for Behavioral Change
13. Groupthink's Impact on Decision-Making
14. Influence of Cognitive Functions
15. Cognitive Bias
16. Avoiding Cognitive Bias
17. Critical Thinking
18. Measurement of Critical Thinking skills
19. Improving Critical Thinking Skills
20. Benefits of Thinking Slow
21. The Dilemma of Logical Decision
22. Measuring how we think
23. Logical Reasoning
24. Reasons why logic is crucial in daily life
25. Key Behaviours of a Logical Thinker
26. Are you solving the right problems?
27. Pitfalls of Problem-solving in Business
28. Typical Problems According to Personality Types
29. Applying MBTI Advantage for Success

30. Problem-Solving Strategies
31. Data-Driven Decision Making
32. Benefits of Data-Driven Decision-Making
33. Strategies for Embracing a Data-Centric Approach
34. AI-based decision-making tools
35. Seven steps for effective decision-making.
36. Frameworks for Intelligent Decision-Making
37. Addressing Wrong Decisions

Elevate your analytical prowess and confidently tackle challenges through this comprehensive guide.

**Book 3 Grow Creative Mindset**

**Are you ready to awaken your creative genius, navigate uncharted territories, and craft innovative solutions by exploring inventive thinking and adaptability in problem-solving?**

Embark on an enlightening journey with 'Grow Creative Mindset,' the third book in the 'Successful Intelligence' series. Delve into Sternberg's Triarchic Theory, exploring the depths of experiential intelligence, novelty creativity, and practical adaptation. *Unleash your innate creative potential through exercises and strategies designed to amplify your imaginative prowess, problem-solving finesse, and adaptability in ever-evolving scenarios.*

**This book will take you on an exhilarating journey through the following key topics, unraveling intriguing insights-**
1. Creative Mindset
2. Triarchic Theory of Intelligence
3. Creative Intelligence
4. Creative Thinking in Business
5. Personality Types and Cognitive Functions
6. Potential Environment of Creativity
7. Science Behind Creativity
8. Cognitive Functions of Idealists

9. Creative Personality Traits
10. Contradictory Traits of Creative Individuals
11. Enemy of Creativity
12. Are you a creative person?
13. Managerial Practices Affecting Creativity
14. Why We Struggle with Creativity
15. Minimalism for Creativity
16. Importance of Creativity in Business
17. Creativity at Workplace
18. AI-Enabled Automation and Creative Intelligence
19. Global Creativity Dynamics
20. Boosting Your Innovative Potential
21. Creativity and Design Thinking
22. Steps to Foster Creativity in Your Organization
23. 12 Types of Innovation Strategies
24. Ideation Process
25. 10 Effective Ideation Techniques
26. The transformative power of creative thinking
27. The Potential of Your Creativity
28. Qualification points for a good idea
29. Steps to Convert Ideas into Reality
30. Creativity and Successful Intelligence

Elevate your cognitive landscape and tap into the boundless realms of creativity with this transformative guide.

## Fearless Empathy Series

### Book 1 : Set Smart Boundaries

**"Want to find the answers to the questions holding you back?** *Ask yourself these five questions:*

1. Are you tired of feeling like a pushover in your personal and professional relationships? It's time to take control and set clear boundaries in the workplace.
2. Are you fed up with constantly giving in to others' demands and not standing up for yourself? Let's work on developing

assertiveness skills in your personal and professional life.
3. Do you need help communicating your needs and wants confidently and effectively in your personal and professional life? Let's explore ways to improve your assertiveness.
4. Are you feeling drained and unappreciated in your personal and professional relationships? It may be time to take a hard look at how you set and enforce your boundaries.
5. Are you ready to take charge of your life and start living in alignment with your values in your personal and professional life? Let's work on building your assertiveness and boundary-setting skills.

"**Set Smart Boundaries:** is a comprehensive guide for anyone looking to improve their relationships, advance their career, and achieve their goals. **This book provides a specific, measurable, achievable, realistic, and time-bound approach to setting boundaries.** The natural ability to set boundaries is different for everyone. Certain people must consciously impose it as they cannot set boundaries naturally. In the MBTI 16Personality types, Intuitive & Sensory Feelers, require training in setting limits. Get ready for an eye-opening adventure as this book takes you on a journey through the subtopics below, unravelling intriguing insights and captivating stories.

1. Why Spot Takers?
2. Definition of Boundaries
3. Who should set boundaries?
4. How to spot takers?
5. Toxic behaviours in people.
6. Why learn mindful giving?
7. Material Boundaries
8. Financial Boundaries
9. Givers & Takers
10. Why start valuing yourself?
11. Social Boundaries
12. Workplace boundaries

13. Religious and Intellectual Boundaries
14. Why should we protect our vibes?
15. Social Media Boundaries
16. How can we create social media boundaries?
17. How to build boundaries with mobile phones?
18. How to build boundaries with online meetings or classes?
19. How can we prevent abuse?
20. Personal Boundaries
21. Cyber Bullying
22. Sexual Boundaries
23. Why Stop being taken for granted?
24. Time-based Boundaries
25. Trauma Response
26. Signs of Poor Boundaries
27. Signs of being taken for granted
28. Traits prone to be taken advantage of
29. How can you stop people from taking advantage of you?
30. Exceptions to SMART Boundaries

This book is packed with practical advice, actionable tips, and real-life examples to help you set the boundaries you need to achieve success and happiness. Whether you're dealing with a demanding boss, a toxic friend, or a controlling partner, "Set Smart Boundaries" provides a step-by-step approach to help you take control of your life, career, and relationships.

**Book 2 : Master Mindful No**

**Are you tired of feeling overwhelmed in a world that never stops demanding your attention?**
Ask yourself these five questions:
1. Do you feel like you're constantly distracted and putting other people's needs ahead of your own, even if it means sacrificing your well-being? Let's Identify if you're a people pleaser and break free from this habit, prioritizing your needs for a fulfilling life.

2. Do you struggle with being true to yourself and practicing self-care? Let's discover practical ways to practice real self-care and be more authentic for a more fulfilling life.
3. Are your fears holding you back from achieving your goals and living your best life? Let's explore your concerns and move forward with confidence and purpose.
4. Do you struggle with managing guilt and difficulties when you say "no"? Let's strategize for managing guilt and difficulties that may arise when speaking "no" to maintain healthy relationships and confidence.
5. Have you ever struggled with saying "no" without damaging your relationships or professional reputation? Let's Learn to say "no" positively and effectively, prioritizing our own needs while respecting the needs of others.

"Master Mindful No" offers practical strategies to help you filter distractions, overcome manipulation, and eliminate fear and guilt to succeed in a constantly demanding environment.
<u>The natural ability to say No is different for everyone. Certain people must consciously learn it as they cannot be assertive naturally. In the MBTI 16Personality types, Intuitive & Sensory Feelers require training in prioritizing their needs.</u>
This book takes you through the subtopics below, unraveling intriguing insights and captivating stories.
1. What is Mindfulness?
2. What is Mindful 'No'?
3. What is Distraction?
4. Why are we distracted?
5. Types of Distractions
6. Cost of Distraction
7. Practicing Mindful 'No' with Distractions
8. Root Causes of People Pleasing Behaviour
9. Courage Vs. Warmth
10. Manipulation Definition.

11. Signs of Manipulation
12. Practicing Mindful No with Manipulation.
13. What is Authenticity?
14. Authenticity and Sincerity
15. How to be Authentic?
16. Cost of Authenticity
17. Cons of authenticity at work.
18. Are your values limited?
19. Is fear what is standing in your way?
20. Why do we fake fear?
21. What are the common fake fears? How can we move forward?
22. Signs that you are living in fear
23. Mindfulness to transform fear.
24. Present-day fears of our life
25. Definition of Guilt
26. Shame Vs. Guilt
27. Shaming
28. Overcoming Guilt
29. Managing Guilt at Work
30. Guilt and Shame as Marketing Tools
31. Principles of Positive No
32. Power of Positive No in Negotiations
33. Saying No as a Productivity Hack
34. How to Say Positive No
35. Saying No at Work

With practical exercises, real-life examples, and thought-provoking insights, "Master Mindful No" is the ultimate resource <u>for anyone who wants to learn how to say "no" mindfully, with confidence and purpose.</u> Whether you're struggling with people-pleasing tendencies or feeling overwhelmed by commitments, this book will help you navigate the complexities of modern life and live a more fulfilling, peaceful life.

## Book 3: Conquer Key Conflicts

**"Do you crave to break free from the relentless cycle of adjustment?"**
Ask yourself these five pivotal questions:

1. Are you tired of avoiding conflicts and arguments and ready to develop the courage to face them head-on? Assess your growth values.
2. Are you seeking practical strategies to transform conflicts into opportunities? Uncover opportunities for success.
3. Do you want to understand the benefits of conflicts and learn how to manage them effectively? Navigate for positive outcomes.
4. Are you ready to choose healthy battles and leave your comfort zone? Discover more authentic answers.
5. Do you want constructive confrontation? Foster a positive attitude and deepen relationships.

"Conquer Key Conflicts" offers 7 **Effective Strategies** to Stop Avoiding Arguments, Develop the Courage to Disagree, and Achieve Deserving Results in a Challenging Environment.

The natural ability to face conflicts is different for everyone. Certain people must consciously learn it as they cannot be assertive naturally. In the MBTI 16Personality types, Intuitive & Sensory Feelers require training in prioritizing their needs.
 Discover a transformative guide to navigating conflicts with confidence and achieving excellent results. Explore the drawbacks of conflict avoidance, unlock the potential benefits of conflicts, and learn to choose healthy battles. This book takes you through the subtopics below, unraveling intriguing insights with examples.
1. Definition of Conflict
2. Triggers of Conflicts
3. Types of Conflict
4. Personality Types & Values
5. Values of MBTI Types
6. Personal Value Conflicts
7. What is Conflict Avoidance?
8. Signs of Conflict Avoidance

9. Conflict Avoidance or Value imbalance?
10. Values for growth
11. Result of Conflict Avoidance in Organisation.
12. Tips for Overcoming Conflict Avoidance
13. Should we encourage conflicts?
14. Disagreeing at work
15. Advantages of Conflicts at Work
16. Merits of Difficult Conversations
17. Conflict of Interest
18. Examples of Conflict of Interest at Work
19. Differentiating Conflicts
20. Arguments to Avoid
21. Choosing Value Conflicts for Success
22. Supporting the Right People in Conflicts
23. Conflicts and their Roots
24. Effective Confrontation
25. Mindful Confrontation
26. Tips for Constructive Confrontation.
27. Impact of Communication on Conflict Resolution
28. Effective Communication Strategies for Constructive Confrontation.
29. Importance of Active Listening
30. Applications & Benefits of Active Listening
31. Conflict Management Skills
32. Thomas-Kilmann Conflict Mode Instrument
33. Strategies for Value-based Conflict Resolution
34. Systems for Managing Workplace Conflicts
35. The Seven Strategies to Conquer Key Conflicts

From understanding the nature of disputes to **embracing healthy confrontation**, this book takes you on a journey of self-discovery and empowerment. *With practical strategies for resolution, you'll develop the courage to disagree and achieve positive outcomes in any challenging environment.*

**Book 4: Build Emotional Resilience**

**Are you tired of being swept away by the chaos of**

life, losing your balance in the turbulence?
*Ask yourself these five questions:*
1. What if you could navigate life's challenges without being overwhelmed? Get ready to rewrite your relationship with adversity.
2. Have you ever felt your emotions spinning out of control? Dive into the heart of emotional imbalance and discover the tools to regain control.
3. What if you could break free from emotional dependence? Explore the empowering merits of emotional independence and learn how to cultivate it.
4. Can emotions indeed be your allies? Gain the power to make informed decisions and forge a more authentic path.
5. What if you could gracefully dance through life's ups and downs? Discover how to cultivate this invaluable skill and watch as life's challenges transform into opportunities for growth.

Step into emotional reinforcement, where you'll learn how to nurture and magnify the emotions that uplift you. This is your guide to mastering Emotional Resilience and thriving in chaos. *With captivating stories, practical exercises, and eye-opening insights, this book is your companion on the journey to a calmer, more empowered you.*

The innate capacity to process emotions varies among individuals. Some people may need to consciously develop this skill, especially if they possess heightened sensitivity. According to the MBTI 16 Personality Types, individuals categorized as Intuitive and Sensory Feelers may benefit from acquiring Emotional Resilience through training. This book takes you through the subtopics below, unraveling intriguing insights and captivating stories.

1. Emotional Resilience
2. Emotional Intelligence Vs. Emotional Resilience
3. Factors Influencing Emotional Resilience
4. Negative Emotions
5. Emotional Setbacks
6. Relevance of Emotional Resilience

7. People Vulnerable to Frequent Emotional Imbalance
8. Highly Sensitive Persons (HSPs) and Empaths
9. Emotional Imbalance and Energy
10. Emotional Imbalance Based on Personality Type Cognitive Functions
11. Emotional Imbalance Based on Trauma
12. Emotional Independence
13. Ways to Achieve Emotional Independence
14. The Power of Detachment
15. The Power of Non-Reaction
16. Emotions are built, not built-in
17. Three Ways to Better Understand Your Emotions
18. Premeditatio Malorum
19. The Theory of Constructed Emotions
20. Strategies for Emotional Intelligence at Work
21. The Science of Romantic Love
22. Three Methods to manage emotions in the workplace
23. Habits of Emotionally Disciplined Leaders
24. Emotional Agility
25. Radical Acceptance of Emotions
26. Measuring Emotional Agility and Resilience
27. Emotional Agility for Workplace Success
28. Emotional Agility for Effective Leadership
29. Shame Resilience Therapy
30. Resilience in the Face of Harsh Criticism
31. Energy Frequencies, Emotions, and Healing
32. 9 Strategies for Lifting Your Mood Immediately:
33. Tips for Naturally Boosting Energy Levels
34. 10 Ways to Enhance Emotional Resilience
35. The Healing Power of Connection
36. Holistic Approaches to Emotional Resilience and Well-being

*This book unveils the intelligence hidden within your emotions and teaches you how to harness their wisdom. Emotional Resilience is your ticket to fluidly adapting to any situation.*

## Book 5: Develop Vital Connections

Are you weary of navigating the ruthless battleground of modern life without a safety net?
Ask yourself these pivotal questions:

1. What if you could harness the power of effective communication and self-expression to overcome life's challenges confidently? Understand the profound impact of connections on your growth, happiness, and success.
2. Have you ever considered the advantages of a robust support system in our competitive world? Discover the benefits of nurturing personal and professional relationships.
3. Struggling to establish vital connections? Learn to identify and conquer common barriers that hold you back.
4. How can you choose connections that elevate your life? Gain the wisdom to cultivate relationships that truly empower you.
5. Need techniques for lasting connections? Equip yourself with practical strategies to build meaningful bonds.

Step into vital connections, where you'll learn the art of mastering effective communication, empowering your self-expression, and enhancing your value in this competitive arena. *This book isn't just a guide; it's your steadfast companion on the journey toward a more connected, thriving you.*
<u>Innate connection-making abilities differ among individuals. Some may need to develop this skill, especially if they prefer solitude consciously. According to MBTI's 16 Personality Types, Introverted Intuitives can benefit from strengthening their connection-building skills.</u>
In a world where the ability to build and maintain vital

connections is your golden ticket to success, whether you're a natural social butterfly or someone who could use a bit of extra guidance, **"Develop Vital Connections" reveals the intelligence concealed within the craft of connection-building, teaching you how to harness its incredible potential.**

This book will take you on an exhilarating journey through the following key topics, unraveling intriguing insights and sharing captivating stories:
1. Vital Connections
2. Attachment Styles
3. Factors of Connections for Growth
4. Effective Communication vs. Self Expression
5. The Power of Networks
6. Connecting with a Common Story
7. Connections for Opportunities and Job Advancement
8. Connections to Enhance Learning and Knowledge Sharing
9. Amplifying Influence Through Meaningful Connections
10. Connections to Console and Navigate Challenges or Distress Times
11. Connections to Fulfil Life
12. Introverts and Extroverts
13. Why do Introverts Avoid Small Talk?
14. Why Do Some People Avoid Socializing?
15. How Trust Issues Impact Communication
16. The Connectedness Corrective
17. Inability to Identify the Value of Communication
18. Chances for Establishing Connections
19. Building Meaningful Connections for Your IKIGAI
20. Connections for Adapting to Change
21. Balancing Patience and Proactivity
22. What is the reason behind our innate drive for connection?
23. Knowing Personality Types for Connection

24. What Is Effective Communication?
25. Mastering Effective Communication
26. Communication Tips for Maximum Impact
27. The Power of 'Because' to Influence Behavior
28. Gesticulation and Nonverbal Cues in Effective Communication
29. How to Make People Feel Heard?
30. Building Lasting Connections
31. Authentic Connections
32. 10 Effective Ways to Build Solid Professional Connections
33. Three Predictors of Lasting Connections

Join us on this transformative adventure and witness your life evolve into a tapestry woven with flourishing connections, boundless opportunities, and unwavering support.

**Clear Career Inclusive Series**

**Book 1: Raising Your Rare Personality**

***Find who you are to be your best!***
What is your personality type? Are you the right fit for your career? Who is a rare personality type? This book provides all the answers. Psychology is the scientific study of mind and behavior. Understand how psychology defines your unique type, growth potential, and suitable careers. Myers-Briggs Type Indicator (MBTI), a tool to identify personality typology, classifies people into 16Personalities. You can belong to any one of these 16 personality types based on your psychological preferences. Some personality types are stated as rare personality types as per MBTI. The personality type INFJ has been explored in-depth in this book. The purpose of this book is to show solidarity to who you are, identify suitable careers for all MBTI types, with a focus on the rare personality types.

**Key Learnings from the book - Raising Your Rare Personality**

## Chapter 1 MBTI Personality Types
1. What are MBTI Personality Types?
2. How can you understand your Personality Type?
3. What are the 16Personalities?
4. Who are Rare Personality Types?
5. Who is the Rarest Personality Type?

## Chapter 2 MBTI Cognitive Functions
1. What are Cognitive Functions?
2. What are the 8 Cognitive Functions?
3. What is a Primary Cognitive Function?
4. What is a Shadow Cognitive Function?
5. Cognitive Functions of all MBTI Personality Types

## Chapter 3 INFJ Primary Cognitive Experiences
1. What are the Primary Cognitive Functions of an INFJ?
2. How does Introverted Intuition behave?
3. How does Extraverted Feeling behave?
4. How does Introverted Thinking behave?
5. How does Extraverted Sensing behave?

## Chapter 4 INFJ Shadow Cognitive Experiences
1. What are the Shadow Cognitive functions of an INFJ?
2. How does Extroverted Intuition behave?
3. How does Introverted Feeling behave?
4. How does Extroverted Thinking behave?
5. How does Introverted Sensing behave?

## Chapter 5 Rare Personality Types and Growth
1. Growth potential Function of MBTI Personality Types.
2. What are Functional Pairs?
3. How Intuition works in Rare Personality Types?
4. Strength and Weakness of INFJ Personality Types
5. Famous Personalities of all MBTI Rare Personality Types

## Chapter 6 Careers for your Personality
1. Functional Pair strength for all Personality Types
2. Careers for Intuitive Feelers
3. Careers for Intuitive Thinkers
4. Careers for Sensory Feelers
5. Careers for Sensory Thinkers

## Resources
Free Test links for finding MBTI Personality, Enneagram, Socionics, Big 5, DISC, Holland Code Job Aptitude Test, etc. are included in the book.

"A man's true delight is to do the things he was made for."
– Marcus Aurelius
✓ **Find Yours!**

**Book 2: Upgrade as Futuristic Empaths**

*Find your strength to give your best!*
Are you an empath? Do you know what an empathy trap is? How can you transform empathy into a strength and build successful careers?
**Empaths** have intuitive feelings (owing to the cognitive functional pair "NF" in their personality type) as their psychological preference. Personality types ENFP, ENFJ, INFJ, and INFPs are natural empaths as per the **MBTI Personality types** according to www.16personalities.com and www.Truity.com. Empaths are also called **Idealists & Diplomats. Highly Sensitive People** belong to these MBTI types. To face the realities of the world and to be successful in endeavours which have larger impacts, empaths need to embrace practicality and rise above their personality stereotype or one-sidedness.
Dr.Dario Nardi, Author of the book **Neuroscience of Personality**, suggests transcendence or the individuation process, a term coined by **Carl Jung**, the essence of which is to have an integrated personality growth. Empaths have a larger role to play in this world and most of them are underplaying their natural strength.
*By adopting the 5 key steps discussed in this book, anyone, especially empaths can easily find their career paths to success, thereby leaving a positive impact on this world.*

*Key Learnings from the book - Upgrading as Futuristic Empaths.*
**Chapter 1 Understanding Empaths**
1. Empathic People or Empaths
2. Empathy Dilemma
3. The Value of Empathy
4. Practising Empathy
5. The Empathy Trap

6. Use of Empathy in day-to-day life
7. Empathy and Business
8. Empathy and Leadership

**Chapter 2 Finding your Strength**
1. Empath's Strength, Weakness & Dilemma
2. Empaths as Employees
3. Clifton Strengths
4. Machiavelli's Dilemma
5. Empath's Choice
6. Empathy as a strength in daily life
7. Fearless Empathy
8. Nurturing Empathy

**Chapter 3 Developing Your Profile**
1. An Empath's Growth Cognitive Function
2. Moving from One-sidedness to individuation
3. Challenges of One-sidedness for Empaths
4. The Magic Diamond for Integrated/Transcendent Judgement & Perception
5. Preferred Growth of Empaths Cognitive Functions
6. The Spiral Development of Cognitive Functions
7. Using Empathy as a Strength
8. Essentials for Building an Empath's Profile
9. Careers and Majors for Empaths

**Chapter 4 Finding Your Market Niche**
1. Sustainable Development Goals in Business
2. Future Job Skills
3. Selecting a Career for Empaths
4. Challenges of Workplace Toxicity
5. Future of Jobs for Empaths
6. Empaths and the Gig Economy

**Chapter 5 Connecting & Networking**
1. The Power of Social Connection
2. Why are we not Connecting?
3. Impact of Networking
4. Managing Digital Distraction

**Chapter 6 Creating Opportunities**
1. Opportunities for Empathy in Business
2. Opportunities in Sustainability

3. Empathy Revolution

*"Objective judgment, now, at this very moment. Unselfish action, now, at this very moment. Willing acceptance — now, at this very moment — of all external events. That's all you need." - Marcus Aurelius*
✓ **Find How!**

**Book 3: Onboard as Inclusive Leaders**

***Find Your Potential to Impact the Best!***
How Inclusive are you? Are you unconsciously biased?
Do you promote Psychological Safety?
This book will help you find answers and enable you *Onboard as Inclusive Leaders.*
**Innovation, financial performance and employee productivity** are indispensable for business growth.
Inclusion helps in achieving these objectives of business. Diversity in line with inclusion and equity creates a sense of belonging in employees.
This book helps to develop the essential qualities required to be hired as an inclusive leader; **understand unconscious biases, the importance of psychological safety and how it has an impact on workplace productivity.**
The book also gives you the free test links to understand your MBTI personality type, strength, and Bias Tests (The Implicit Association test - Harvard University)

**Key Learnings from the book:**
**Chapter 1 Knowing Inclusion**
1. Why do we need Inclusive Leaders?
2. What is an Inclusive Workplace?
3. Features of an Inclusive Workplace
4. Challenges of Inclusive Workplace
5. Merit based Inclusion
6. Who is an inclusive leader?

**Chapter 2 Inclusion Gap**
1. Facts of Diversity & Inclusion
2. Microaggression

3. Unconscious Bias
4. 16 Unconscious Biases
5. Bias Test (The Implicit Association Test)
6. The Cost of Unconscious Bias

**Chapter 3 Inclusion in Practice**
1. Inclusion in the workplace
2. Inclusion Strategies at Ingersoll Rand
3. Inclusion Mandate
4. Expectations of Gen Z
5. Disability Inclusion
6. LGBTQ+ Inclusion
7. Six Signature Traits of Inclusive Leaders
8. Risks of Casual Diversity Programs

**Chapter 4 Inclusion Participants**
1. Types of Inclusion
2. Physical Inclusion
3. Psychological Inclusion
4. Importance of Assertiveness for Empaths at work
5. Empathy and Neuroscience of Personality Types
6. Preparing the Team for Inclusion

**Chapter 5 Inclusion Process**
1. Inclusion Strategy
2. Psychological safety
3. International Standards for Inclusion Process
4. Inclusive Job Posting
5. Inclusive Hiring
6. DEI Interview Questions
7. Disparate Treatment & Disparate Impact

**Chapter 6 Inclusion Measurement**
1. Measurement of Inclusion
2. Gartner Inclusion matrix
3. How Inclusive is your leadership?
4. Fundamental Interpersonal Relations Orientation (FIRO®)
5. Empathy & Inclusion Measurement
6. Industry Measurement of Diversity & Inclusion

*"If someone can prove me wrong and show me my mistake in any thought or action, I shall gladly change. I*

*seek the truth, which never harmed anyone: the harm is to persist in one's own self-deception and ignorance."*
— *Marcus Aurelius*

**We need more inclusive leaders who will consider others in their decisions and that alone can give rise to sustainable development and positive impacts for people and the planet.**

✓Find How

# Acknowledgement

My gratitude to the readers of my book, for your time and reviews, and to all my well-wishers for your support. I am indebted to all who reached out to me with feedback and input. I have to start by thanking my family, friends, and classmates for their encouragement, counsel, and good-natured jibes. Extending my wholehearted gratitude to everyone on the Author Freedom Hub, special thanks to Som Bathla for his vote of confidence and my fellow authors for their unbounded support. To Anita Jocelyn for her editorial help towards the completion of my book. I am grateful to Mr. Sareej for his efforts towards the beautiful cover design. I thank my friends and colleagues who helped me with their insights and experiences of their work place inclusion. Your inputs were critical in the completion of this book and helped me gather information to cover this topic in details for my readers. In no way at all the least, I am very thankful to my spouse Jo and our son Yakob for helping me out immensely by allowing me space and time to pursue my interests and creating a conducive environment to achieve my goals. To my mother Prof. Thresiamma Sunny, I am thankful for her unwavering support and inspiration to always deliver my best.

I could not have done it without you all.

# References

Chapter 1

1. Israel - Facts, History & Conflicts | HISTORY
2. Freud's Id, Ego, and Superego: Definition and Examples (verywellmind.com)
3. Carl Jung – The Balance of Personality (pressbooks.pub)
4. The 8 Jungian Functions: Roles, Images & Characteristics (personalityjunkie.com)

Chapter 2

1. Joker: A Powerful Psychological Drama | Psychology Today
2. Hidden personality - Wikipedia
3. The hidden side to your personality - BBC Future
4. Conscientiousness: Meaning, Signs, and Effects on Behavior (verywellmind.com)
5. Neuroticism: Definition, Traits, Causes, and Ways to Cope (simplypsychology.org)
6. Personal unconscious - Wikipedia
7. An Introduction to the Shadow Functions - Psychology Junkie
8. Face Your Dark Side - Carl Jung and the Shadow - YouTube
9. What Are The Four Sides Of The Mind? | C.S. Joseph (csjoseph.life)

Chapter 3

1. The Psychology of Socialism and Capitalism | Psychology Today
2. How to Use Power, Influence, and Persuasion for Good | Psychology Today
3. Projection | Psychology Today

4. Nardi, Dario. The Magic Diamond: Jung's 8 Paths for Self-Coaching (p. 55). Radiance House. Kindle Edition.

## Chapter 4

1. Personality Development Tools: The Car Model – Personality Hacker
2. Nardi, Dario. The Magic Diamond: Jung's 8 Paths for Self-Coaching (p. 78). Radiance House. Kindle Edition.
3. What Is Individuation in Psychology? (verywellmind.com)

## Chapter 5

1. Navaratri - Wikipedia
2. What is shadow work? Benefits and exercises (medicalnewstoday.com)
3. The Beauty and Brilliance of Shadow Work | Psychology Today
4. 7 Powerful Shadow Work Techniques and Practices (subconsciousservant.com)
5. 100+ Deep Shadow Work Prompts To Accept Yourself And Move Forward (scienceofpeople.com)
6. Is Shadow Work Dangerous? A Comprehensive Look at the Pros and Cons (thesmartread.com)

## Chapter 6

1. The Truth About the INFJ Door Slam (introvertdear.com)
2. Yin and Yang: How Ancient Ideas of Balance Can Help You (verywellmind.com)
3. Masculine vs. Feminine Energy Explained: What Are They? (wikihow.com)
4. Balancing Personality Traits: Capitalizing on the strengths of our "true self" - FFI Practitioner
5. DUALITY – The Importance of Finding BALANCE In Your Identity - DR. LOGAN JONES (drloganjones.com)

**Copyright © 2024 by Devi C.Sunny**

All Rights Reserved. No part of this book may be reproduced or used in any manner without the written permission of the copyright owner except for the use of quotations in a book review.

Printed in Great Britain
by Amazon